Python for Robotics

Programming Intelligent Machines Develop robotic applications using Python and machine vision

THOMPSON CARTER

Table of Content

TABLE OF CONTENTS

Introduction

Python for Robotics: Programming Intelligent Machines

In the realm of modern technology, robotics stands as one of the most transformative fields, driving innovation across various industries, from healthcare and manufacturing to logistics and space exploration. At the heart of this technological revolution lies **Python**, a powerful yet accessible programming language that has become the go-to tool for building intelligent machines. **"Python for Robotics: Programming Intelligent Machines"** aims to bridge the gap between theory and practical implementation, guiding readers through the intricacies of programming robotic systems using Python.

As robotics systems become more autonomous, flexible, and intelligent, the need for robust and intuitive programming tools has grown. Python, with its simplicity, readability, and extensive ecosystem of libraries, has emerged as the preferred language for robotics developers. Whether it's building machine learning algorithms for autonomous decision-making, controlling robotic arms in industrial settings, or using computer vision for object recognition, Python has proven to be a versatile and efficient language in the world of robotics.

This book provides both **beginners** and **experienced developers** with a comprehensive understanding of robotics and how to apply Python to build real-world robotic applications. It explores core concepts of robotics, such as sensor integration, motion control, kinematics, and machine vision, while also delving into more advanced topics like AI, machine learning, and reinforcement learning in robotics.

Why This Book is Important

Robotics, once a niche area for specialized engineers and researchers, is rapidly becoming accessible to a broader audience. The rapid advancements in automation, AI, and machine learning are enabling robots to perform increasingly complex tasks autonomously. As robotics evolves, the programming tools we use need to adapt to new challenges and capabilities. Python, with its simple syntax and powerful libraries, is perfectly suited to meet these challenges, making it an essential skill for anyone aspiring to work in robotics.

While there are other programming languages used in robotics, Python's ability to interface with cutting-edge technologies such as machine learning frameworks (TensorFlow, PyTorch), robotic simulation tools (Gazebo, V-REP), and real-time operating systems (ROS) makes it the ideal language for building intelligent systems. Python also offers an extensive community, robust documentation, and an abundance of libraries that simplify tasks such as controlling sensors, processing images, and handling data from robotic systems.

What You Will Learn

Core Robotics Concepts: We will introduce you to the foundational concepts of robotics, including understanding robotic hardware, sensors, actuators, and the basic components that make up a robotic system. You'll learn how Python interacts with these components to control movement, collect data, and perform tasks.

Motion Control and Kinematics: In robotics, controlling the movement of machines is crucial. We will dive into kinematics—both forward and inverse kinematics—and how Python can be used to program robot motion, ensuring that your robots can navigate the world effectively and with precision.

Machine Vision: Vision plays a vital role in many robotic applications, from autonomous vehicles to industrial inspection systems. This book introduces you to **machine vision** concepts, utilizing Python libraries like OpenCV, enabling robots to "see" their environment, detect objects, and make informed decisions.

Advanced Robotics Algorithms: You will explore how Python is used in advanced robotics algorithms, such as **reinforcement learning**, **path planning**, and **robot navigation**. These techniques will allow robots to adapt, learn, and optimize their actions based on real-world feedback.

AI and Deep Learning in Robotics: Python is widely used for integrating AI and deep learning models into robotics systems. In this book, we will cover how to apply deep learning for tasks like object recognition, speech processing, and autonomous decision-making, helping you build smarter robots.

Practical Real-World Applications: Throughout the book, we will provide practical examples and case studies, showcasing how Python is used in industries such as **healthcare, manufacturing**, and **space exploration**. We'll also look at **real-time control systems, robotic simulation**, and **robot-to-human interaction**, ensuring that you can apply what you learn in real-world projects.

Who This Book is For

This book is intended for anyone interested in learning how to program robots using Python, whether you're just starting out or you're already familiar with Python and want to apply your skills in robotics. It's perfect for:

- **Students and Aspiring Engineers**: If you are pursuing a career in robotics or automation, this book provides a strong foundation to get started with programming intelligent robots.
- **Developers Transitioning into Robotics**: If you have experience in software development but want to dive into robotics, this book will equip you with the necessary tools to integrate Python into your robotic projects.
- **Hobbyists and Makers**: Whether you're working with a DIY robot kit or experimenting with robotic systems at home, this book will guide you through the process of

programming robots with Python in a way that's easy to understand and implement.

How to Use This Book

The book is structured to take you step-by-step through the learning process, starting with fundamental topics and gradually progressing to more advanced concepts. Each chapter builds upon the previous one, allowing you to develop your knowledge and skills at your own pace. The examples provided are practical and tailored to real-world scenarios, ensuring that you not only understand the theory but also gain hands-on experience.

You will find **exercises** and **examples** throughout the book, which encourage you to apply what you have learned to actual coding projects. By the end of the book, you will have built several simple yet powerful robotic systems using Python and be well on your way to exploring more complex robotics applications.

Conclusion

"Python for Robotics: Programming Intelligent Machines" serves as both an introduction to the field of robotics and a practical guide for developing real-world robotic applications using Python. Whether you're learning robotics from scratch or looking to expand your programming expertise, this book will provide you with the knowledge and skills you need to succeed.

The world of robotics is rapidly advancing, and Python is one of the driving forces behind its progress. This book will not only equip you with the technical knowledge to develop robots, but also inspire you to take part in the exciting future of robotics, from autonomous systems to AI-powered machines.

By the end of this book, you will have the tools and insights to begin building your own intelligent robotic systems using Python and gain the confidence to explore even more advanced concepts and applications in the field of robotics. Let's dive in and begin your journey into the fascinating world of robotics!

CHAPTER 1

INTRODUCTION TO ROBOTICS AND PYTHON

Overview of Robotics: What It Is, Types of Robots, and Their Applications

Robotics is the branch of technology that deals with the design, construction, operation, and use of robots. A robot can be defined as a machine designed to carry out a series of actions automatically, either autonomously or semi-autonomously. These machines are created to perform tasks that are typically repetitive, dangerous, or difficult for humans to carry out.

Types of Robots:

- **Industrial Robots**: These are used in manufacturing processes, like assembly lines, packaging, and welding. They are designed to handle heavy loads with precision and speed.

- **Autonomous Mobile Robots (AMRs)**: These robots navigate and perform tasks without human intervention, using sensors, cameras, and other technologies for autonomous decision-making. Examples include delivery robots and autonomous cars.

- **Humanoid Robots**: These robots resemble the human body and are designed to interact with people or perform tasks similar to human capabilities. Boston Dynamics' Atlas is a prime example of humanoid robots.
- **Medical Robots**: Used for surgeries, patient care, or rehabilitation. Robotic surgery systems like the Da Vinci Surgical System fall into this category.
- **Service Robots**: These robots are used in non-industrial settings like homes, restaurants, or hotels. Examples include robot vacuum cleaners and reception robots.
- **Research Robots**: These are used in scientific research, space exploration, and other fields where high precision and sophisticated sensors are needed.

Each type of robot has a specific role, and Python can be used to program and control them effectively.

Introduction to Python: Why Python Is a Preferred Language for Robotics

Python has become one of the most popular programming languages in the world of robotics, and for several good reasons:

- **Ease of Use**: Python's syntax is simple and easy to learn, making it ideal for both beginners and experienced programmers. This helps roboticists focus on solving problems rather than dealing with complex syntax.
- **Extensive Libraries and Frameworks**: Python has a rich ecosystem of libraries and frameworks, many of which are tailored specifically for robotics. Libraries like OpenCV for computer vision, TensorFlow for machine learning, and PyRobot for robotics make it easier to develop complex robotic systems.
- **Integration with Other Technologies**: Python integrates well with various platforms and hardware used in robotics, like Raspberry Pi, Arduino, and ROS (Robot Operating System). This integration is essential for controlling robots in real-world environments.
- **Community and Support**: The Python community is vast, and there's an abundance of resources, tutorials, forums, and open-source projects that make it easier to find solutions to specific problems in robotics.

15

Setting Up Your Python Environment: Installing Necessary Libraries and Tools

To begin programming robots with Python, setting up the appropriate environment is crucial. Here's a step-by-step guide:

1. **Install Python**: Download the latest version of Python from the official Python website. Ensure you add Python to your system's PATH during installation.

2. **Install Code Editor/IDE**: While you can use any text editor, a full-fledged Integrated Development Environment (IDE) will make coding easier. Some popular Python IDEs for robotics include:

   o **PyCharm**

   o **VS Code**

   o **Thonny (for beginners)**

3. **Install Libraries**: Use `pip` (Python's package manager) to install libraries that are essential for robotics. Some must-have libraries for robotics include:

   o `numpy`: For numerical operations, a common need in robotics algorithms.

   o `opencv-python`: For machine vision tasks like object detection and image processing.

o `RoboPi` or `RPi.GPIO`: For interfacing with hardware like Raspberry Pi.

o `rospy`: For programming robots with ROS. To install libraries, open your command-line interface (CLI) and type:

```
nginx
```

```
pip install numpy opencv-python rospy
```

4. **Setting Up ROS (Robot Operating System)**: ROS is an open-source operating system that provides tools for controlling robots. Install ROS on your system by following the instructions on the official ROS website.

5. **Connecting Hardware**: Ensure your robot's hardware (e.g., motors, sensors, cameras) is properly set up. Use platforms like Raspberry Pi or Arduino to interface with these components. Python can be used to control and read data from sensors, actuators, and cameras.

Real-World Examples: How Python is Used in Robotics

Python is widely used in robotics for both simple and complex tasks. Here are a few examples of how it is implemented in real-world robotics:

17

1. **Controlling Motors with Python**: A robot with a set of motors that need to move in specific directions can be controlled using Python. For example, using the `RPi.GPIO` library, you can write code to turn a robot left, right, forward, or backward based on input from sensors or pre-programmed instructions.

2. **Vision-Based Object Detection**: Python, combined with the `OpenCV` library, is used in robotic vision. A robot with a camera can capture images or video, then analyze the data to identify objects, obstacles, or even people. For instance, a robot used in a warehouse may use Python to recognize and pick up packages.

3. **Autonomous Navigation**: Python plays a crucial role in autonomous navigation for robots. With libraries like `numpy` for mathematical computations and `rospy` for communication with ROS, Python can be used to program algorithms that enable robots to navigate around obstacles, map environments, and make decisions on their path.

4. **Robot Arm Control**: Python can control robotic arms in applications like 3D printing or picking and placing objects. Using Python, you can write scripts

18

to control the servos, adjust the arm's position, and coordinate movements to perform precise tasks.

5. **Simulation and Testing**: In research and development, Python is used in simulation environments such as Gazebo to simulate how a robot will behave in a real-world scenario. Developers use Python to code the robot's responses to different conditions and test its performance before deploying it.

By using Python in these real-world scenarios, robotics developers can create powerful, efficient, and flexible systems.

This chapter sets the stage for the rest of the book, helping readers understand the basics of robotics and the role Python plays in it. It also equips them with the tools and libraries they'll need to get started with robotics programming.

CHAPTER 2

BASIC PYTHON CONCEPTS FOR ROBOTICS

Variables, Loops, Functions, and Data Structures in Python

Before diving into robotics programming, it's essential to have a solid understanding of basic Python concepts. These foundational concepts will help you write clean and efficient code for controlling robotic systems.

Variables: In Python, variables are used to store data. Python is dynamically typed, meaning you don't need to declare the type of a variable explicitly. Here's how to create a variable:

```python
robot_speed = 5
```

In this example, `robot_speed` is a variable that stores the speed of a robot, and the value 5 is an integer.

Loops: Loops are used to repeat actions multiple times. In robotics, loops can be useful for continuous tasks like reading sensor data or controlling a robot's movements over time.

- **For Loop**: Typically used when you know how many times you want to repeat an action.

python

```python
for i in range(5):
    print("Move forward")
```

- **While Loop**: Used when you want to repeat an action until a certain condition is met.

python

```python
while robot_speed < 10:
    robot_speed += 1
    print(f"Speed increased to {robot_speed}")
```

Functions: Functions are blocks of reusable code that can be executed when called. In robotics, functions can be used to encapsulate specific tasks like turning the robot, moving it forward, or reading data from sensors.

python

```
def move_forward(speed):
    print(f"Moving forward at speed {speed}")

move_forward(5)
```

In this case, the `move_forward()` function takes a parameter (`speed`) and executes the corresponding action.

Data Structures: Python provides several types of data structures to store and organize data:

- **Lists**: Ordered collections of items.

```python
```

```
robot_commands = ["move forward", "turn left",
"move backward"]
```

- **Dictionaries**: Key-value pairs, ideal for storing data that is paired together.

```python
```

```
robot_position = {"x": 0, "y": 0}
```

- **Tuples**: Immutable ordered collections.

```python
```

```
robot_state = ("moving", "speed: 5")
```

These data structures can help manage complex data related to robot control, like positions, commands, or sensor readings.

Python's Object-Oriented Approach: Classes and Objects

Python is an object-oriented programming (OOP) language, which means it allows you to model real-world entities using classes and objects.

Classes: A class is a blueprint for creating objects. It defines attributes (data) and methods (functions) that the objects created from it will have.

python

```python
class Robot:
    def __init__(self, name, speed):
        self.name = name
        self.speed = speed

    def move_forward(self):
        print(f"{self.name} is moving forward at
speed {self.speed}")
```

In this example:

- The `__init__` method is a special function that is called when a new object is created. It initializes the object's attributes, such as `name` and `speed`.
- The `move_forward()` method defines a behavior for the robot.

Objects: An object is an instance of a class. You can create an object by calling the class as if it were a function.

```python
python
```

```python
robot1 = Robot("Robot1", 5)
robot1.move_forward()  # Output: Robot1 is moving
forward at speed 5
```

In this case, `robot1` is an object of the `Robot` class. You can create as many objects (robots) as you need, each with different attributes and behaviors.

Object-oriented programming makes it easier to organize complex systems, such as robotics, into smaller, manageable pieces.

Example: Simple Python Script for Controlling a Robot's Basic Movement

Now that we've covered basic Python concepts, let's put them into practice with a simple Python script to control a robot's basic movement. In this example, we'll simulate a robot's movement using functions, loops, and object-oriented principles.

python

```python
class Robot:
    def __init__(self, name, speed):
        self.name = name
        self.speed = speed
        self.position = {"x": 0, "y": 0}

    def move_forward(self):
        self.position["y"] += 1
        print(f"{self.name} is moving forward. Current position: {self.position}")

    def move_backward(self):
        self.position["y"] -= 1
        print(f"{self.name} is moving backward. Current position: {self.position}")

    def turn_left(self):
```

```
        self.position["x"] -= 1
        print(f"{self.name} turned left. Current
position: {self.position}")


    def turn_right(self):
        self.position["x"] += 1
        print(f"{self.name}      turned      right.
Current position: {self.position}")


# Create a robot object
robot1 = Robot("Robo", 5)


# Move the robot forward and backward
robot1.move_forward()
robot1.move_forward()


# Turn the robot left and right
robot1.turn_left()
robot1.turn_right()
```

Explanation:

- We created a `Robot` class with a constructor (`__init__`) that initializes the robot's name, `speed`, and `position`.
- We defined movement functions (`move_forward`, `move_backward`, `turn_left`, `turn_right`) that update the robot's position on a 2D plane.

- We created an instance of the `Robot` class (`robot1`) and called the movement functions to simulate the robot's movement.

Output:

pgsql

```
Robo is moving forward. Current position: {'x':
0, 'y': 1}
Robo is moving forward. Current position: {'x':
0, 'y': 2}
Robo turned left. Current position: {'x': -1,
'y': 2}
Robo turned right. Current position: {'x': 0,
'y': 2}
```

This chapter covered basic Python concepts like variables, loops, functions, data structures, and object-oriented programming (OOP). By understanding these concepts, you can effectively control a robot's movements, manage its data, and structure complex robotics systems. The example script provided demonstrates how to use these concepts to create a simple robot control system.

CHAPTER 3

UNDERSTANDING ROBOTICS HARDWARE

Overview of Essential Robotic Components (Motors, Sensors, Actuators)

In robotics, various hardware components work together to perform tasks autonomously or under human control. Understanding these components is essential for programming robots and controlling their actions. Let's explore the key components of robotics: motors, sensors, and actuators.

Motors: Motors are one of the most critical components in robotics because they provide the power needed for movement. There are several types of motors used in robotics:

- **DC Motors**: These motors are simple and commonly used in small robots. They rotate continuously when powered and are great for driving wheels or propellers.

- **Servo Motors**: These are used for precise control of angular position. Servo motors are often found in robotic arms, allowing for accurate and controlled movements.
- **Stepper Motors**: These motors move in discrete steps, making them ideal for applications where precise control of position is needed, such as in 3D printers or CNC machines.

Sensors: Sensors provide feedback to robots, enabling them to perceive their environment. Some common sensors used in robotics include:

- **Ultrasonic Sensors**: Used for distance measurement by emitting sound waves and measuring the time it takes for the sound to reflect back.
- **Infrared Sensors**: Used for proximity detection or simple object tracking by detecting infrared light.
- **Camera Sensors (Vision)**: Cameras and image sensors enable robots to "see" and analyze their surroundings. These are particularly useful in machine vision and image recognition tasks.
- **Gyroscope and Accelerometer**: These sensors measure orientation and acceleration, helping robots maintain balance or navigate their environment.

Actuators: Actuators are devices that convert energy (usually electrical) into physical motion. They are responsible for carrying out the tasks assigned to robots. Common types of actuators include:

- **Linear Actuators**: These actuators produce straight-line motion and are used for pushing or pulling actions.
- **Rotary Actuators**: These actuators provide rotational motion, commonly used in robotic arms or wheels for movement.

Together, these components allow a robot to move, perceive its surroundings, and interact with the environment.

Interfaces Between Hardware and Python

Python is a versatile programming language that can interface with various hardware components in robotics. To control motors, sensors, and actuators, we typically use libraries that allow communication between Python and the hardware, usually via a platform like **Raspberry Pi** or **Arduino**.

Some common interfaces and protocols used to connect Python to robotics hardware include:

- **GPIO (General Purpose Input/Output)**: Available on platforms like Raspberry Pi, GPIO pins allow you to control motors, LEDs, and read sensor data.
- **I2C (Inter-Integrated Circuit)**: A communication protocol used for connecting microcontrollers to sensors and other devices.
- **SPI (Serial Peripheral Interface)**: A high-speed communication protocol often used for connecting sensors or actuators to microcontrollers.
- **Serial Communication (UART)**: Often used to send and receive data between a computer and a microcontroller (e.g., using USB or Bluetooth).

Python libraries like `RPi.GPIO` (for Raspberry Pi) or `pySerial` (for serial communication) provide the tools needed to interface with hardware.

Example: Connecting Python to a Basic Motor Driver

In this example, we'll walk through how to connect a basic motor driver (using an H-bridge) to a Raspberry Pi and control a DC motor. This setup allows you to control the motor's direction and speed via Python.

Hardware Setup:

- **Raspberry Pi**: The microcontroller that will interface with the motor.
- **L298N Motor Driver**: A common motor driver used to control DC motors.
- **DC Motor**: The motor that will be controlled.
- **Power Supply**: To power the motor.
- **Jumper Wires**: For making connections.

Connections:

1. Connect the **IN1** and **IN2** pins from the motor driver to two GPIO pins on the Raspberry Pi (e.g., GPIO 17 and GPIO 18).
2. Connect the **ENA** pin to a 5V pin on the Raspberry Pi (for enabling the motor driver).
3. Connect the **OUT1** and **OUT2** pins to the motor's terminals.
4. Connect the **VCC** and **GND** pins of the motor driver to an external power supply (appropriate for your motor) and the Raspberry Pi's GND.
5. Ensure the motor is powered with the external supply while the Raspberry Pi controls the motor driver.

Python Code: Here's a basic Python script to control the direction and speed of the DC motor using the L298N motor driver and Raspberry Pi GPIO.

```python
python

import RPi.GPIO as GPIO
import time

# Set up GPIO mode
GPIO.setmode(GPIO.BCM)

# Motor Driver Pins
IN1 = 17  # GPIO pin 17 connected to IN1 on L298N
IN2 = 18  # GPIO pin 18 connected to IN2 on L298N
ENA = 22  # GPIO pin 22 connected to ENA on L298N
(for enabling motor)

# Set up GPIO pins as output
GPIO.setup(IN1, GPIO.OUT)
GPIO.setup(IN2, GPIO.OUT)
GPIO.setup(ENA, GPIO.OUT)

# Enable the motor driver
GPIO.output(ENA, GPIO.HIGH)

def move_motor_forward():
    GPIO.output(IN1, GPIO.HIGH)
    GPIO.output(IN2, GPIO.LOW)
    print("Motor is moving forward")

def move_motor_backward():
    GPIO.output(IN1, GPIO.LOW)
```

```python
    GPIO.output(IN2, GPIO.HIGH)
    print("Motor is moving backward")

def stop_motor():
    GPIO.output(IN1, GPIO.LOW)
    GPIO.output(IN2, GPIO.LOW)
    print("Motor stopped")

# Move the motor forward for 5 seconds, then stop
it
move_motor_forward()
time.sleep(5)
stop_motor()

# Move the motor backward for 5 seconds, then
stop it
move_motor_backward()
time.sleep(5)
stop_motor()

# Clean up GPIO settings
GPIO.cleanup()
```

Explanation:

- The script first sets the GPIO pins on the Raspberry Pi for controlling the motor.

- It defines functions to control the motor's movement: `move_motor_forward()`, `move_motor_backward()`, and `stop_motor()`.
- The motor is moved forward for 5 seconds, stopped, then moved backward for 5 seconds, and stopped again.
- The `GPIO.cleanup()` function ensures that the GPIO settings are reset when the program finishes.

Expected Output: The motor will move forward for 5 seconds, stop, move backward for 5 seconds, and then stop again.

This example demonstrates how Python can interface with hardware components (like motors) through GPIO pins on a Raspberry Pi. By using libraries like `RPi.GPIO`, you can easily control a robot's hardware, allowing it to move and interact with the environment. In robotics, such simple scripts can be extended to create more sophisticated control systems for complex robotic applications.

CHAPTER 4

WORKING WITH SENSORS AND ACTUATORS

Introduction to Sensors (Ultrasonic, Infrared, Camera Sensors) and Actuators

Sensors and actuators are fundamental components in any robotic system. Sensors allow robots to "perceive" their environment by gathering data, while actuators enable them to interact with the world by performing actions.

Sensors:

- **Ultrasonic Sensors**: These sensors use sound waves to measure distance. They emit an ultrasonic pulse and then measure the time it takes for the pulse to reflect back from an object. This time is then used to calculate the distance. Ultrasonic sensors are commonly used for obstacle detection and ranging in robotics.
  - *Common Models*: HC-SR04
- **Infrared Sensors**: Infrared (IR) sensors use infrared light to detect obstacles or objects. They either emit infrared

light and measure the reflected light or use passive infrared (PIR) to detect motion or heat sources.

- *Common Models*: IR modules for proximity detection, PIR sensors for motion detection

- **Camera Sensors**: These sensors allow robots to "see" their environment. Cameras can capture images or video, which can then be processed to recognize objects, detect obstacles, or track movements. Camera sensors are commonly used in machine vision and autonomous navigation.

  - *Common Libraries*: OpenCV, PiCamera (for Raspberry Pi)

Actuators:

- **Motors**: As we discussed in the previous chapter, motors are used to provide movement. They can be controlled by Python to drive wheels, control robotic arms, or operate other moving parts.

- **Servos**: These are used for precise control of rotational movement, often in robotic arms or for turning components.

- **Pneumatic and Hydraulic Actuators**: These actuators use pressurized air or fluid to generate movement. While less common in smaller robots, they are used in more complex industrial robots.

- **Linear Actuators**: These provide straight-line motion and are often used for pushing or pulling applications.

Sensors provide feedback to the robot about its environment, while actuators use that data to take action, creating a feedback loop in robotics.

Using Python to Read Data from Sensors

Python is widely used in robotics because of its simplicity and the availability of libraries to interact with various sensors. To interface with hardware like sensors, Python uses the GPIO pins on platforms like Raspberry Pi or Arduino, or it may communicate with microcontrollers over protocols like I2C, SPI, or UART.

Here's how Python can be used to interface with common sensors:

1. **Ultrasonic Sensors**: Python can read the distance by measuring the time it takes for the ultrasonic pulse to return.
2. **Infrared Sensors**: Python can be used to detect the presence of obstacles or measure proximity by reading the output of an IR sensor.

3. **Camera Sensors**: Python, along with libraries like OpenCV, can capture and process images or video streams.

Libraries and Tools:

- `RPi.GPIO` or `gpiozero` (for Raspberry Pi GPIO control)
- `time` (for handling delays in sensor readings)
- `OpenCV` (for image processing with camera sensors)

Example: Interfacing a Distance Sensor with Python

In this example, we'll connect an **HC-SR04 Ultrasonic Distance Sensor** to a Raspberry Pi and use Python to measure the distance to an object. The HC-SR04 ultrasonic sensor has two main pins for communication: **Trigger** and **Echo**.

Hardware Setup:

1. Connect the **VCC** pin to a 5V pin on the Raspberry Pi.
2. Connect the **GND** pin to a GND pin on the Raspberry Pi.
3. Connect the **Trigger** pin to a GPIO pin (e.g., GPIO 17).
4. Connect the **Echo** pin to another GPIO pin (e.g., GPIO 18).

Python Code:

```python
python

import RPi.GPIO as GPIO
import time

# Set up GPIO mode
GPIO.setmode(GPIO.BCM)

# Set up pins for Trigger and Echo
TRIG = 17
ECHO = 18

# Set up GPIO pins
GPIO.setup(TRIG, GPIO.OUT)
GPIO.setup(ECHO, GPIO.IN)

def measure_distance():
    # Send a pulse to the Trigger pin
    GPIO.output(TRIG, GPIO.LOW)
    time.sleep(0.1)
    GPIO.output(TRIG, GPIO.HIGH)
    time.sleep(0.00001)  # Send a short pulse
    GPIO.output(TRIG, GPIO.LOW)

    # Wait for the Echo pin to go HIGH (start of pulse reception)
    while GPIO.input(ECHO) == GPIO.LOW:
```

```
        pulse_start = time.time()

    # Wait for the Echo pin to go LOW (end of
pulse reception)
    while GPIO.input(ECHO) == GPIO.HIGH:
        pulse_end = time.time()

    # Calculate the duration of the pulse
    pulse_duration = pulse_end - pulse_start

    # Calculate the distance (speed of sound is
34300 cm/s)
    distance = pulse_duration * 17150  # distance
in cm
    distance = round(distance, 2)   # Round to 2
decimal places

    return distance

try:
    while True:
        distance = measure_distance()
        print(f"Distance: {distance} cm")
        time.sleep(1)  # Wait for 1 second before
the next measurement

except KeyboardInterrupt:
    print("Measurement stopped by user")
    GPIO.cleanup()  # Clean up GPIO settings
```

Explanation:

- The `measure_distance()` function sends a pulse to the **Trigger** pin to activate the ultrasonic sensor.
- The script then waits for the **Echo** pin to go HIGH, which indicates that the pulse has been reflected back.
- The time difference between the pulse transmission and reception is used to calculate the distance, using the speed of sound (34300 cm/s).
- The program continuously measures the distance and outputs it to the terminal every second.

Expected Output:

```makefile
makefile

Distance: 25.67 cm
Distance: 26.12 cm
Distance: 24.93 cm
...
```

Explanation of Output: The sensor measures the distance to the closest object in front of it, and the program continuously displays the distance in centimeters. The distance updates every second as long as the script runs.

This example demonstrates how to use Python to interface with a simple ultrasonic distance sensor, allowing you to measure the distance to objects. Similar methods can be used with other sensors (IR, camera, etc.) by adjusting the code to match the specific sensor's data reading protocol. This is a key step in enabling robots to perceive their environment and react to changes, whether for obstacle avoidance, navigation, or object manipulation.

CHAPTER 5

INTRODUCTION TO ROS (ROBOT OPERATING SYSTEM)

What is ROS and Why It Is Important in Robotics

The **Robot Operating System (ROS)** is an open-source framework that provides tools and libraries for building robotic applications. Despite its name, ROS is not a traditional operating system but rather a collection of software frameworks for writing robot software. It acts as a middleware that allows different software components to communicate and work together seamlessly, enabling the integration of various hardware components and complex algorithms.

Key Features of ROS:

1. **Modularity**: ROS provides a modular structure where developers can break down a robot's functionalities into smaller, manageable packages. Each package contains code, libraries, and configurations for specific robot behaviors.

44

2. **Communication**: ROS offers several communication methods, including:

   o **Topics**: Used for sending messages asynchronously between different parts of a system (publishers and subscribers).

   o **Services**: Provide synchronous request-response interactions.

   o **Actions**: A combination of topics and services that are used for long-duration tasks.

3. **Hardware Abstraction**: ROS abstracts hardware interfaces, meaning developers can write code for robot sensors, actuators, and controllers without worrying about the specifics of the underlying hardware.

4. **Reusability**: ROS supports reusability of code through open-source packages, meaning many common robotics tasks like navigation, perception, and control already have pre-built solutions.

5. **Visualization Tools**: ROS provides several powerful visualization tools such as **RViz** and **rqt** to visualize robot states, sensor data, and system performance.

6. **Community Support**: Being open-source, ROS has a large and active community that continuously develops and shares tools and libraries for all aspects of robotics.

Because of these features, ROS is widely used in both research and industry for developing complex robotics systems. It provides a standardized platform that allows for interoperability between various components of a robot system, from sensors and actuators to algorithms and control systems.

Setting Up ROS with Python

To use ROS with Python, we need to install **ROS** on your system and configure the environment for Python development. ROS uses a Python client library called `rospy`, which is a part of the ROS ecosystem.

Steps to Set Up ROS with Python:

1. **Install ROS**: Follow the installation instructions for ROS on your system. ROS supports multiple Linux distributions (such as Ubuntu) and macOS. Here's how you would typically install ROS on Ubuntu:

```bash
sudo apt update
sudo apt upgrade
sudo apt install ros-noetic-desktop-full
```

For other operating systems, refer to the official ROS installation guide.

2. **Install Dependencies**: You will need to install Python and some additional ROS dependencies. To do so, run:

    bash

    ```
    sudo apt install python3-pip
    sudo apt install python3-rospy
    sudo apt install ros-noetic-ros-base
    ```

3. **Setup ROS Workspace**: ROS operates within a workspace. You will need to create a workspace for your robot's code. The following commands will create a workspace and initialize it:

    bash

    ```
    mkdir -p ~/catkin_ws/src
    cd ~/catkin_ws
    catkin_make
    source devel/setup.bash
    ```

4. **Set Up Your Python Environment**: ROS uses rospy for Python. You will need to ensure that your Python environment is properly set up to work with

ROS. If you're using Python 3, you may need to install `ros-noetic-rospy` and configure Python to use it.

Real-World Example: Using ROS to Control a Simple Robotic System

Let's look at how to use ROS with Python to control a simple robotic system. In this example, we'll simulate controlling a robot using ROS with Python, focusing on moving the robot forward and backward using **ROS topics**.

Example: Controlling a Robot with ROS and Python

This example assumes that you have ROS installed and a basic setup for controlling a robot's movement through the `cmd_vel` topic (which is commonly used for controlling robots in ROS).

1. **Creating a Python ROS Node**: First, we'll create a ROS node that sends velocity commands to the robot. ROS nodes are programs that perform computations and communicate with other parts of

the system. In this case, the node will publish movement commands to the `cmd_vel` topic.

Python Script (`robot_control.py`):

```python
#!/usr/bin/env python

import rospy
from geometry_msgs.msg import Twist

def move_robot():
    # Initialize the ROS node
    rospy.init_node('robot_control',
anonymous=True)

    # Create a publisher to send velocity
commands
    pub = rospy.Publisher('/cmd_vel', Twist,
queue_size=10)

    # Set the loop rate (10Hz)
    rate = rospy.Rate(10)

    # Create a Twist message to hold velocity
data
    move_cmd = Twist()
```

```
    # Set the linear speed to move forward and
angular speed to 0 (no rotation)
    move_cmd.linear.x = 0.5   # Move forward at
0.5 m/s
    move_cmd.angular.z = 0.0    # No angular
movement (no rotation)

    rospy.loginfo("Moving robot forward")

    # Publish the command for 5 seconds
    for _ in range(50):  # 50 times at 10Hz = 5
seconds
        pub.publish(move_cmd)
        rate.sleep()

    # Stop the robot after moving forward
    move_cmd.linear.x = 0.0
    rospy.loginfo("Stopping robot")
    for _ in range(50):  # 50 times at 10Hz = 5
seconds
        pub.publish(move_cmd)
        rate.sleep()

if __name__ == '__main__':
    try:
        move_robot()
    except rospy.ROSInterruptException:
        pass
```

Explanation of the Code:

- **rospy.init_node()** initializes the ROS node, allowing it to interact with the ROS master.
- **rospy.Publisher()** creates a publisher that sends messages to the cmd_vel topic. This topic is often used to send velocity commands to robots.
- **Twist** is a message type used for controlling robot velocity. We specify linear.x for forward speed and angular.z for rotational speed.
- The program then sends the velocity command to the robot every 100ms for 5 seconds to move it forward. Afterward, it sets the linear speed to 0.0, stopping the robot.

2. **Running the Script**: To run the script, you'll need to source your ROS setup file and execute the Python script:

bash

```
source ~/catkin_ws/devel/setup.bash
roslaunch your_robot_launch_file.launch
rosrun your_package robot_control.py
```

This will start the robot moving forward for 5 seconds and then stop.

Expected Output: The robot will move forward for 5 seconds and then stop. You can modify the `move_cmd.linear.x` and `move_cmd.angular.z` values to change the robot's speed and direction.

This simple example demonstrates how ROS can be used with Python to control a robot's movement through the `cmd_vel` topic. By publishing velocity commands and subscribing to topics that report sensor data, you can create more complex behaviors for robots, including obstacle avoidance, navigation, and task execution.

ROS is a powerful framework for building scalable and modular robotic systems, and with Python's simplicity, it becomes an ideal tool for developing robots quickly and efficiently.

CHAPTER 6

PYTHON FOR MOTION CONTROL IN ROBOTICS

Basics of Motion Control in Robotics: Speed, Distance, and Direction

In robotics, motion control is crucial for enabling a robot to navigate and perform tasks in a controlled manner. Understanding how to control a robot's movement is essential for creating reliable, efficient, and precise robotic systems. Let's break down the fundamental components of motion control: speed, distance, and direction.

Speed: Speed refers to how fast a robot moves. It's typically measured in meters per second (m/s) or other units, depending on the robot's environment. Speed control is important in applications where robots need to move efficiently without overshooting targets or colliding with obstacles.

- **Linear Speed**: The forward or backward speed of the robot, usually controlled by adjusting the motor's rotation speed.
- **Rotational Speed**: The speed at which a robot turns or rotates around an axis. This is typically controlled by adjusting the speed difference between the left and right motors.

Distance: Distance control is the ability to move a robot over a specific distance. To move accurately, robots often rely on feedback mechanisms such as encoders (measuring wheel rotation) or sensors to detect position.

- **Encoders**: These sensors track the rotation of the wheels and can be used to calculate the distance traveled. A simple way of calculating distance is based on the wheel's circumference and the number of rotations.
- **Time-Based Movement**: For basic motion, robots can also use time to approximate the distance traveled based on the speed.

Direction: Direction control refers to the ability to steer a robot. Direction is usually determined by controlling the robot's wheels or actuators in a coordinated manner. In differential drive robots (robots with two wheels), direction is controlled by varying the speed of each wheel:

- **Straight Movement**: Both wheels rotate at the same speed.
- **Turning Left or Right**: One wheel moves faster than the other.

Implementing Motion Control with Python

Python is an excellent language for implementing motion control due to its simplicity and the availability of libraries that interface with robot hardware (like motors and sensors). To implement motion control with Python, you typically need to:

1. Set the desired speed for the motors.
2. Calculate the movement direction (forward, backward, turning).
3. Use sensors or encoders for feedback (if needed).
4. Program the robot to move over the required distance and time.

To control motion, you can use libraries like:

- **RPi.GPIO** or **gpiozero** (for controlling motors and actuators on platforms like Raspberry Pi).

- **PWM (Pulse Width Modulation)**: Used to control motor speed by adjusting the duty cycle of the signal sent to the motor.
- **Encoder Feedback**: To monitor and control distance or speed more accurately.

Example: Programming a Robot to Move in a Square Pattern

In this example, we will create a simple Python script to control a robot's movement in a square pattern. We will use two motors for a differential drive robot. The robot will move forward, turn 90 degrees, repeat the process four times, and complete the square.

For simplicity, let's assume the robot uses two motors controlled via GPIO pins on a Raspberry Pi, and we will simulate the movement without using encoders. We'll base the movement on time for a basic approximation.

Hardware Setup:

- **Motors**: Two DC motors controlled by an H-Bridge motor driver (e.g., L298N).
- **GPIO pins**: Connect the motor driver's input pins to the Raspberry Pi's GPIO pins for controlling motor direction and speed.

Python Code:

```python

import RPi.GPIO as GPIO
import time

# Set up GPIO mode
GPIO.setmode(GPIO.BCM)

# Motor driver pins (assuming L298N H-Bridge)
IN1 = 17  # Motor 1 direction pin
IN2 = 18  # Motor 1 direction pin
IN3 = 22  # Motor 2 direction pin
IN4 = 23  # Motor 2 direction pin
ENA = 24  # Enable pin (for motor speed control)

# Set up GPIO pins as output
GPIO.setup(IN1, GPIO.OUT)
GPIO.setup(IN2, GPIO.OUT)
GPIO.setup(IN3, GPIO.OUT)
GPIO.setup(IN4, GPIO.OUT)
GPIO.setup(ENA, GPIO.OUT)

# Enable the motor driver
GPIO.output(ENA, GPIO.HIGH)

# Function to move the robot forward
def move_forward():
```

```python
    GPIO.output(IN1, GPIO.HIGH)
    GPIO.output(IN2, GPIO.LOW)
    GPIO.output(IN3, GPIO.HIGH)
    GPIO.output(IN4, GPIO.LOW)
    print("Moving forward")

# Function to turn the robot 90 degrees (turn
right)
def turn_right():
    GPIO.output(IN1, GPIO.HIGH)
    GPIO.output(IN2, GPIO.LOW)
    GPIO.output(IN3, GPIO.LOW)
    GPIO.output(IN4, GPIO.HIGH)
    print("Turning right")

# Function to stop the robot
def stop_robot():
    GPIO.output(IN1, GPIO.LOW)
    GPIO.output(IN2, GPIO.LOW)
    GPIO.output(IN3, GPIO.LOW)
    GPIO.output(IN4, GPIO.LOW)
    print("Stopping")

# Main loop to move the robot in a square pattern
try:
    for _ in range(4):  # Repeat 4 times for a
square
        move_forward()
```

```
        time.sleep(2)    # Move  forward  for  2
seconds (adjust time for distance)
        stop_robot()
        time.sleep(1)    #  Short  pause  before
turning
        turn_right()
        time.sleep(1)    #  Turn  for  1  second
(adjust for 90 degrees)
        stop_robot()
        time.sleep(1)  # Short pause before next
movement

except KeyboardInterrupt:
    print("Program interrupted by user")

finally:
    GPIO.cleanup()  # Clean up GPIO settings
```

Explanation of the Code:

- **move_forward()**: This function sets both motors to move the robot forward. The GPIO pins are configured to make both motors rotate in the forward direction.
- **turn_right()**: This function turns the robot by making one motor rotate forward and the other backward (differential drive principle).
- **stop_robot()**: Stops the robot by setting all motor pins to LOW.

- The main loop runs the robot forward for 2 seconds, stops it for 1 second, turns right for 1 second, and repeats this four times to complete a square pattern.

Expected Output:

- The robot will move forward, then turn 90 degrees, repeat this process four times, and complete a square pattern.

This example demonstrates basic motion control by programming a robot to follow a square pattern. The speed and turning angles are approximated based on time. For more precise control, you can use sensors like encoders to track the distance or feedback loops to fine-tune the robot's movement.

Python provides a powerful and simple way to control motion in robotics. By using libraries like `RPi.GPIO`, you can interface with motors and sensors to create more advanced motion control systems for complex robotic applications.

CHAPTER 7

KINEMATICS AND FORWARD/INVERSE KINEMATICS

Explanation of Kinematics in Robotics: Position and Motion

Kinematics in robotics refers to the study of motion without considering the forces that cause that motion. It is essential in robotics because it helps us understand how a robot moves and how different parts of a robot's body or arm can be controlled to achieve a desired position or movement.

Position: Position refers to the location of a robot or a part of the robot (like an arm or wheel) in space. It is typically represented using coordinates (x, y, z) in 2D or 3D space. In robotics, knowing the position of a robot allows us to determine where it is in its environment and where it needs to go.

Motion: Motion describes how the robot or its parts move. For example, how a robotic arm rotates or how a mobile robot moves along a path. Motion is typically represented by linear motion (movement along a straight line) and angular motion (rotation around an axis).

Kinematics helps us calculate how changes in the robot's joints or wheels affect its overall position and orientation in space. There are two main types of kinematics in robotics: **forward kinematics** and **inverse kinematics**.

Forward and Inverse Kinematics in Python

Forward Kinematics: Forward kinematics involves calculating the position and orientation of the end-effector (the part of the robot that interacts with the environment, such as the hand of a robotic arm) based on known values for the robot's joints (angles, lengths, etc.). Forward kinematics is useful when you know the joint parameters and want to determine the robot's position in space.

For a robotic arm with multiple joints, forward kinematics involves applying transformation matrices (which describe the motion of the joints) to calculate the end-effector's position.

Inverse Kinematics: Inverse kinematics is the reverse of forward kinematics. Given a desired position and orientation for the end-effector, inverse kinematics is used to calculate the joint angles required to achieve that position. This is a more complex problem because there may be multiple ways to reach the same position, and solving for the joint angles often requires numerical methods.

In practice, inverse kinematics is crucial for tasks like robotic arm manipulation, where you want to place the arm in a specific location to pick up an object.

Real-World Example: Programming a Robot Arm's Movement

Let's consider a robotic arm with two joints (elbow and shoulder) and a gripper (end-effector). We want to use Python to control the arm's movement based on forward and inverse kinematics. We'll simulate the motion of the robotic arm using forward kinematics to calculate the end-effector's position and inverse kinematics to determine the joint angles required for a given position.

In this example, we'll assume that the arm's structure is as follows:

- **Shoulder joint**: Rotates around the base (theta1).
- **Elbow joint**: Rotates around the first link (theta2).
- **Gripper**: At the end of the second link.

Forward Kinematics: For simplicity, let's assume the arm has two links (lengths 11 and 12). The forward kinematics can be expressed using the following equations:

- `x = 11 * cos(θ1) + 12 * cos(θ1 + θ2)`
- `y = 11 * sin(θ1) + 12 * sin(θ1 + θ2)`

Where:

- θ1 is the angle of the shoulder joint (rotation around the base).
- θ2 is the angle of the elbow joint (rotation around the first link).
- 11 and 12 are the lengths of the arm segments.

Inverse Kinematics: The goal of inverse kinematics is to calculate the joint angles θ1 and θ2 given the desired position (x, y) of the end-effector. To solve for these angles, we use trigonometry:

- `θ2 = acos((x^2 + y^2 - 11^2 - 12^2) / (2 * 11 * 12))`

- θ_1 = atan2(y, x) - atan2(l2 * sin(θ_2), l1 + l2 * cos(θ_2))

This gives us the angles required to reach a target position (x, y).

Python Code Example: Forward and Inverse Kinematics for a 2D Robotic Arm

Let's write Python code that calculates both forward and inverse kinematics for a simple 2D robotic arm.

python

```python
import math

# Lengths of the robot arm links
l1 = 10   # Length of the first link (shoulder to elbow)
l2 = 10   # Length of the second link (elbow to gripper)

# Forward Kinematics: Given angles (θ1, θ2),
calculate the position (x, y)
def forward_kinematics(theta1, theta2):
    x = l1 * math.cos(math.radians(theta1)) + l2
* math.cos(math.radians(theta1 + theta2))
```

```python
    y = l1 * math.sin(math.radians(theta1)) + l2
* math.sin(math.radians(theta1 + theta2))
    return x, y


# Inverse Kinematics: Given position (x, y),
calculate the angles (θ1, θ2)
def inverse_kinematics(x, y):
    # Calculate θ2 (elbow joint angle)
    cos_theta2 = (x**2 + y**2 - l1**2 - l2**2) /
(2 * l1 * l2)
    if abs(cos_theta2) > 1:  # If out of reachable
range
        raise ValueError("Target position is out
of reach.")
    theta2 = math.degrees(math.acos(cos_theta2))


    # Calculate θ1 (shoulder joint angle)
    k1 = l1 + l2 * math.cos(math.radians(theta2))
    k2 = l2 * math.sin(math.radians(theta2))
    theta1 = math.degrees(math.atan2(y, x) -
math.atan2(k2, k1))


    return theta1, theta2


# Test with some angles
theta1 = 45  # Shoulder angle in degrees
theta2 = 30  # Elbow angle in degrees


# Forward Kinematics: Calculate (x, y)
```

```
x, y = forward_kinematics(theta1, theta2)
print(f"Forward Kinematics: x = {x:.2f}, y =
{y:.2f}")


# Inverse Kinematics: Calculate angles (θ1, θ2)
for a given position
target_x = 15
target_y = 10


try:
    theta1,              theta2              =
inverse_kinematics(target_x, target_y)
    print(f"Inverse      Kinematics:      θ1    =
{theta1:.2f}°, θ2 = {theta2:.2f}°")
except ValueError as e:
    print(e)
```

Explanation of the Code:

- **Forward   Kinematics**:   The   function
  forward_kinematics() calculates the position (x,
  y) of the end-effector given the joint angles θ1 and θ2
  using the kinematic equations.
- **Inverse   Kinematics**:   The   function
  inverse_kinematics() calculates the joint angles θ1
  and θ2 required to reach a target position (x, y). It uses
  trigonometric formulas to solve for the joint angles.

Expected Output:

```yaml
```

```
Forward Kinematics: x = 14.14, y = 10.00
Inverse Kinematics: θ1 = 45.00°, θ2 = 30.00°
```

This example demonstrates how to use forward and inverse kinematics to control a robotic arm. By implementing these kinematic models, you can program a robot arm to reach specific positions in space, a fundamental skill for many robotic applications, from assembly to medical procedures.

In real-world scenarios, more complex robots (with more joints or additional degrees of freedom) would require more sophisticated kinematic models. However, the principles of forward and inverse kinematics remain essential for controlling any robotic system.

CHAPTER 8

INTRODUCTION TO MACHINE VISION

What is Machine Vision, and How Does It Relate to Robotics?

Machine vision refers to the ability of a computer or robot to interpret and understand the visual world, usually through the use of cameras or other imaging devices. In robotics, machine vision enables robots to perceive their environment, identify objects, track movement, and make decisions based on visual input, mimicking human sight.

Machine vision plays a vital role in various robotic applications, including:

- **Object recognition**: Identifying and classifying objects within the robot's environment (e.g., picking up items, sorting, or placing).
- **Obstacle detection**: Identifying objects or barriers to avoid collisions while navigating or manipulating objects.

- **Tracking**: Following objects or people to provide feedback for tasks such as motion control or autonomous navigation.
- **Quality control**: In industrial robots, machine vision is used for inspecting products to ensure they meet specific standards.

In robotics, machine vision systems typically consist of cameras (e.g., RGB, depth, or thermal cameras), image processing algorithms, and sometimes machine learning models. These systems allow robots to interact with and understand their surroundings, enabling them to perform tasks that would otherwise require human intervention.

Installing and Setting Up OpenCV for Python

OpenCV (Open Source Computer Vision Library) is a powerful, open-source computer vision library widely used for image and video processing. It provides functions for tasks such as image manipulation, object detection, and feature recognition. OpenCV is ideal for robotics applications that require machine vision.

To get started with machine vision in Python, you'll first need to install OpenCV.

Step 1: Install OpenCV You can install OpenCV using Python's package manager, `pip`. Run the following command in your terminal or command prompt:

```bash
```

```
pip install opencv-python
```

This command installs the core OpenCV package, which includes most of the essential functionality for image and video processing.

Step 2: Install Additional Libraries (Optional) If you need additional features such as working with video streams or using advanced machine learning models, you might want to install the full package:

```bash
```

```
pip install opencv-contrib-python
```

This package contains extra functionality such as specialized algorithms and more advanced image processing tools, useful in more complex vision applications.

Example: Capturing and Processing Images with Python

Let's start with a simple example: capturing images from a webcam and applying basic image processing using OpenCV.

In this example, we'll use OpenCV to capture an image from the webcam, convert the image to grayscale, and display it.

Python Code: Capturing and Processing Images with OpenCV

```python
import cv2

# Initialize the webcam (0 is usually the default
camera)
cap = cv2.VideoCapture(0)

# Check if the camera is opened correctly
if not cap.isOpened():
    print("Error: Could not open video stream.")
    exit()

# Capture images in a loop
while True:
    # Read a frame from the webcam
```

```
    ret, frame = cap.read()

    # Check if the frame was captured correctly
    if not ret:
        print("Error: Failed to capture image.")
        break

    # Convert the image to grayscale
    gray_frame        =        cv2.cvtColor(frame,
cv2.COLOR_BGR2GRAY)

    # Display the original frame
    cv2.imshow("Original", frame)

    # Display the grayscale frame
    cv2.imshow("Grayscale", gray_frame)

    # Wait for the user to press 'q' to quit
    if cv2.waitKey(1) & 0xFF == ord('q'):
        break

# Release the webcam and close any OpenCV windows
cap.release()
cv2.destroyAllWindows()
```

Explanation:

1. `cv2.VideoCapture(0)`: Initializes the webcam. The argument 0 refers to the default camera. If you have multiple cameras, you can change this to 1, 2, etc.

2. `cap.read()`: Captures a frame (image) from the webcam.

3. `cv2.cvtColor(frame, cv2.COLOR_BGR2GRAY)`: Converts the captured color image (in BGR format) into a grayscale image.

4. `cv2.imshow()`: Displays the original image and the grayscale image in separate windows.

5. `cv2.waitKey(1)`: Waits for 1 millisecond for a key press. If the 'q' key is pressed, the loop breaks and the program ends.

Expected Output:

- The program will open two windows:
  - One displaying the original webcam feed.
  - Another displaying the grayscale version of the feed.
- The program will continuously update the images and show them in real-time.
- Press the 'q' key to exit the loop and close the windows.

Basic Image Processing with OpenCV

Now that we can capture and display images, let's explore some basic image processing techniques that are commonly used in robotics.

1. Thresholding: This process converts a grayscale image into a binary image, where pixels are either black (0) or white (255). Thresholding is useful in object detection and segmentation.

python

```python
# Apply binary thresholding
_, binary_frame = cv2.threshold(gray_frame, 127, 255, cv2.THRESH_BINARY)
cv2.imshow("Binary", binary_frame)
```

2. Edge Detection: Using the Canny edge detection algorithm, we can highlight the edges of objects in an image.

python

```python
# Apply Canny edge detection
edges = cv2.Canny(gray_frame, 100, 200)
cv2.imshow("Edges", edges)
```

3. Contour Detection: Contours are useful for shape detection and object recognition. You can use contours to find the boundaries of objects in an image.

python

```
# Find contours
contours,  _  =  cv2.findContours(binary_frame,
cv2.RETR_EXTERNAL, cv2.CHAIN_APPROX_SIMPLE)

# Draw contours on the original frame
cv2.drawContours(frame, contours, -1, (0, 255,
0), 2)
cv2.imshow("Contours", frame)
```

These basic image processing techniques are just the beginning. OpenCV offers a vast array of tools for more advanced vision tasks like object tracking, motion detection, facial recognition, and much more.

Conclusion

Machine vision is a critical component in enabling robots to understand and interact with their environments. By using libraries like OpenCV, Python can be used to easily implement and experiment with various computer vision techniques, allowing robots to perform tasks like object recognition, tracking, and motion control.

In this chapter, we introduced machine vision, explained how to set up OpenCV for Python, and provided a hands-on example of capturing and processing images. With these basic tools, you can begin integrating machine vision into your own robotics projects to create more intelligent, autonomous systems.

CHAPTER 9

OBJECT DETECTION AND RECOGNITION

Basics of Object Detection and Its Importance in Robotics

Object detection is the process of identifying and locating objects within an image or video stream. In robotics, object detection allows a robot to recognize and interact with objects in its environment, which is crucial for tasks such as navigation, manipulation, and quality control.

Object detection involves two key steps:

1. **Classification**: Identifying what the object is (e.g., a cup, a ball, a person).
2. **Localization**: Determining where the object is within the image, often represented by bounding boxes around the detected object.

Why Object Detection is Important in Robotics:

- **Autonomous Navigation**: Robots need to detect and avoid obstacles in their path. For example, a robot vacuum cleaner uses object detection to avoid furniture while cleaning.

- **Manipulation and Grasping**: Robots can use object detection to locate objects they need to pick up or manipulate. This is vital for warehouse robots or robotic arms.

- **Human-Robot Interaction**: In collaborative environments, robots can detect humans or recognize specific gestures to ensure safe interactions.

- **Inspection and Quality Control**: In industrial settings, robots equipped with object detection can inspect products on an assembly line, detecting defects or missing components.

With the rise of machine learning, modern object detection can leverage deep learning algorithms for more accurate and efficient detection, even in complex environments with varying lighting and backgrounds.

Using Python and OpenCV for Object Detection

OpenCV provides various tools and algorithms for object detection. You can perform simple object detection using techniques like:

- **Template Matching**: A technique where a smaller image (template) is matched against a larger image.
- **Haar Cascades**: A machine learning-based approach used to detect objects in images. Often used for face detection.
- **Feature Matching**: Techniques like SIFT (Scale Invariant Feature Transform) and SURF (Speeded Up Robust Features) are used to detect key features in images for object recognition.

Key Libraries in Python:

- **OpenCV**: Provides built-in functions for object detection, such as template matching, feature detection, and Haar cascades.
- **NumPy**: Often used alongside OpenCV for image manipulation.
- **TensorFlow / PyTorch**: Used for implementing deep learning-based object detection models like YOLO (You Only Look Once) or SSD (Single Shot Multibox Detector), which are more advanced methods.

In this chapter, we'll focus on a simpler approach using OpenCV for object detection. Specifically, we'll use **Haar Cascade Classifiers** for detecting objects such as faces, which can be extended to other types of objects.

Real-World Example: Building a Simple Object Detection System

In this example, we will create a basic object detection system using OpenCV to detect faces in real-time using a webcam. We will use a **Haar Cascade Classifier** for face detection, which is a popular method for detecting faces in images.

Step 1: Installing OpenCV

If you haven't already installed OpenCV, you can do so using `pip`:

bash

```
pip install opencv-python
```

Step 2: Downloading Haar Cascade Classifier

Haar Cascade Classifiers are pre-trained classifiers that detect objects in images based on features. OpenCV provides several pre-trained classifiers, including one for face detection.

You can download the **Haar Cascade XML file** for face detection from OpenCV's GitHub repository:

- Haar Cascade Classifier for Face Detection

Save the file **haarcascade_frontalface_default.xml** in your project directory.

Python Code: Detecting Faces in Real-Time Using OpenCV

```python
import cv2

# Load the pre-trained Haar Cascade Classifier
for face detection
face_cascade                                    =
cv2.CascadeClassifier('haarcascade_frontalface_
default.xml')

# Initialize the webcam (0 for the default
webcam)
cap = cv2.VideoCapture(0)

# Check if the webcam is open correctly
if not cap.isOpened():
    print("Error: Could not open video stream.")
    exit()
```

```
# Capture video frames in a loop
while True:
    # Read a frame from the webcam
    ret, frame = cap.read()

    # Convert the frame to grayscale (required
for face detection)
    gray            =           cv2.cvtColor(frame,
cv2.COLOR_BGR2GRAY)

    # Detect faces in the frame using the
face_cascade
    faces = face_cascade.detectMultiScale(gray,
scaleFactor=1.1, minNeighbors=5, minSize=(30,
30))

    # Draw a rectangle around each face detected
    for (x, y, w, h) in faces:
        cv2.rectangle(frame, (x, y), (x + w, y +
h), (255, 0, 0), 2)  # Rectangle in blue

    # Display the frame with the detected faces
    cv2.imshow("Face Detection", frame)

    # Wait for the user to press 'q' to quit the
loop
    if cv2.waitKey(1) & 0xFF == ord('q'):
        break
```

```
# Release the webcam and close OpenCV windows
cap.release()
cv2.destroyAllWindows()
```

Explanation of the Code:

1. **Loading the Haar Cascade Classifier**: The `cv2.CascadeClassifier()` function loads the pre-trained classifier for face detection. The classifier uses XML files that contain the feature data for detecting faces.

2. **Capturing Video Frames**: The `cv2.VideoCapture(0)` function initializes the webcam, and `cap.read()` captures frames from the video stream.

3. **Grayscale Conversion**: The face detection algorithm works on grayscale images, so we use `cv2.cvtColor()` to convert each captured frame to grayscale.

4. **Detecting Faces**: The `detectMultiScale()` function detects faces in the grayscale image. It returns a list of rectangles, each representing a detected face. The parameters `scaleFactor`, `minNeighbors`, and `minSize` fine-tune the detection process.

5. **Drawing Rectangles**: For each face detected, we use `cv2.rectangle()` to draw a blue rectangle around the face.

6. **Displaying the Frame**: The `cv2.imshow()` function displays the frame with the detected faces.

7. **Exiting the Program**: The program exits when the user presses the 'q' key.

Expected Output:

- A window will appear showing the webcam feed with rectangles drawn around detected faces.
- If no faces are detected, the webcam feed will appear without rectangles.
- Press 'q' to exit the program.

Conclusion

In this chapter, we explored the basics of object detection and how it plays a critical role in robotics. We used Python and OpenCV to build a simple real-time face detection system using a Haar Cascade Classifier. Object detection is a key component in robotics, enabling robots to identify and interact with objects, navigate autonomously, and perform complex tasks like picking up objects, following humans, or inspecting items.

As you continue developing more complex robotic systems, machine vision and object detection will be vital for enabling your robots to perform sophisticated, real-world tasks. You can extend this example to detect different objects or integrate deep learning models for more advanced object detection techniques.

CHAPTER 10

IMAGE PROCESSING FOR ROBOTICS

Understanding Image Processing and Its Applications in Robotics

Image processing is the technique of manipulating images to extract useful information or enhance their quality. In robotics, image processing is crucial because it enables robots to "see" and interpret their environment, which is vital for tasks like navigation, object recognition, and manipulation.

Applications of Image Processing in Robotics:

1. **Obstacle Avoidance**: Robots use image processing to detect and avoid obstacles in their path. For example, a robot vacuum uses cameras or depth sensors to map the room and navigate around furniture.

2. **Object Recognition and Tracking**: Image processing allows robots to identify and follow objects. This is essential in applications like warehouse robots, robotic arms, or even humanoid robots.

3. **Visual Servoing**: In this technique, a robot's movement is controlled based on visual feedback. It is commonly used in robotic arms for tasks like pick-and-place operations.

4. **Environmental Mapping**: Image processing helps robots understand their surroundings, creating maps based on visual information, which is essential for autonomous navigation.

5. **Face and Gesture Recognition**: Robots can use image processing for human-robot interaction, identifying faces or gestures to enable more intuitive communication.

By processing images, robots can make decisions, plan their movements, and interact intelligently with the world around them.

Key Techniques in Image Processing: Thresholding, Filtering, and Edge Detection

There are several key image processing techniques that are frequently used in robotics:

1. **Thresholding**: Thresholding is the process of converting a grayscale image into a binary image (black and white). It is commonly used for separating objects from the background.

- o **Simple Thresholding**: Converts pixel values above a certain threshold to white (255) and below it to black (0).
- o **Adaptive Thresholding**: In cases where lighting conditions vary across the image, adaptive thresholding adjusts the threshold for different regions of the image.

2. **Filtering**: Image filtering is used to modify an image by reducing noise, enhancing details, or applying effects. Common types of filters include:

- o **Gaussian Blur**: Reduces image noise and detail by smoothing.
- o **Median Filtering**: Useful for removing noise, especially "salt-and-pepper" noise in an image.
- o **Kernel-Based Filters**: These filters apply a kernel (a small matrix) to each pixel, modifying the pixel's value based on the surrounding pixels.

3. **Edge Detection**: Edge detection identifies boundaries or changes in intensity within an image. It is crucial for tasks like object detection and segmentation.

- o **Canny Edge Detection**: A popular edge detection algorithm that identifies the edges by detecting areas of rapid intensity change.
- o **Sobel Operator**: Detects edges in specific directions (horizontal and vertical).

These techniques are fundamental for enabling robots to process visual data efficiently and extract useful information from images.

Example: Implementing Basic Image Filtering Techniques Using Python

Let's implement basic image filtering techniques using Python and OpenCV. In this example, we will:

1. Apply **Gaussian Blur** to reduce noise.
2. Use **Median Filtering** to remove salt-and-pepper noise.
3. Detect edges using the **Canny Edge Detection** method.

Step 1: Installing OpenCV

If you haven't installed OpenCV yet, you can do so with `pip`:

bash

```
pip install opencv-python
```

Step 2: Python Code for Basic Image Filtering Techniques

python

```python
import cv2
import numpy as np

# Load an image from file
image = cv2.imread('image.jpg')

# Check if the image was loaded correctly
if image is None:
    print("Error: Could not load image.")
    exit()

# Convert the image to grayscale (required for
some processing)
gray_image          =          cv2.cvtColor(image,
cv2.COLOR_BGR2GRAY)

# Apply Gaussian Blur to reduce noise
blurred_image = cv2.GaussianBlur(gray_image, (5,
5), 0)

# Apply Median Filtering to remove salt-and-
pepper noise
median_filtered_image                           =
cv2.medianBlur(gray_image, 5)

# Apply Canny Edge Detection
edges = cv2.Canny(gray_image, 100, 200)
```

```
# Display the original image, blurred image, and
edges
cv2.imshow('Original Image', image)
cv2.imshow('Gaussian Blur', blurred_image)
cv2.imshow('Median        Filtered        Image',
median_filtered_image)
cv2.imshow('Canny Edges', edges)

# Wait until the user presses a key and close all
windows
cv2.waitKey(0)
cv2.destroyAllWindows()
```

Explanation of the Code:

1. **Loading the Image**: The `cv2.imread()` function loads an image from the specified file path. Ensure that the image exists at the given location or the program will not run.

2. **Converting to Grayscale**: The `cv2.cvtColor()` function converts the image from color (BGR) to grayscale, which is often required for many image processing techniques.

3. **Gaussian Blur**: The `cv2.GaussianBlur()` function applies a Gaussian blur to the grayscale image. The `(5, 5)` argument specifies the size of the kernel used for blurring, and `0` is the standard deviation.

4. **Median Filtering**: The cv2.medianBlur() function is applied to remove salt-and-pepper noise. A kernel size of 5 is used, which means it considers a 5x5 neighborhood around each pixel.

5. **Canny Edge Detection**: The cv2.Canny() function detects edges in the grayscale image. The 100 and 200 are the lower and upper threshold values for edge detection. These values can be adjusted for different results.

6. **Displaying the Images**: The cv2.imshow() function displays the original and processed images in separate windows. The program waits for a key press and closes all windows after that.

Expected Output:

- The program will open four windows:
  - The original image.
  - The image after applying Gaussian blur.
  - The image after median filtering.
  - The edges detected by the Canny edge detection algorithm.
- Each window will display the processed image in real-time.

Conclusion

Image processing is a cornerstone of machine vision for robotics, enabling robots to interpret and react to their environment. In this chapter, we explored the importance of image processing and key techniques such as thresholding, filtering, and edge detection. We demonstrated these techniques with a practical Python example using OpenCV, showing how to apply Gaussian blur, median filtering, and edge detection to images.

These basic image processing techniques are the building blocks for more complex tasks in robotics, such as object detection, environment mapping, and autonomous navigation. By leveraging Python and OpenCV, you can begin implementing these techniques in your own robotics applications to enhance your robot's ability to perceive and interact with the world.

CHAPTER 11

MACHINE LEARNING IN ROBOTICS

Introduction to Machine Learning Concepts

Machine Learning (ML) is a subset of artificial intelligence (AI) that enables computers and robots to learn from data and improve their performance over time without being explicitly programmed. Instead of relying on rule-based programming, machine learning models use data to identify patterns, make predictions, and make decisions.

In the context of robotics, machine learning allows robots to:

- **Recognize objects** and classify them.
- **Navigate autonomously** by learning from the environment.
- **Adapt** to changes in the environment or tasks.
- **Optimize decision-making**, allowing robots to perform tasks more efficiently.

There are several key concepts in machine learning:

1. **Supervised Learning**: The model is trained on a labeled dataset, where the input data is paired with the correct output (e.g., image classification with labels).

2. **Unsupervised Learning**: The model works with unlabeled data to find hidden patterns or relationships (e.g., clustering similar objects).

3. **Reinforcement Learning**: The model learns by interacting with the environment and receiving feedback in the form of rewards or penalties (e.g., training a robot to perform a task by trial and error).

4. **Deep Learning**: A subset of machine learning that uses neural networks with multiple layers (deep neural networks) to model complex patterns in large datasets, particularly useful in image and speech recognition.

In robotics, **supervised learning** is often used for tasks like object recognition and classification, while **reinforcement learning** is commonly applied to autonomous navigation and decision-making tasks.

How Python Can Be Used to Implement Machine Learning in Robotics

Python is one of the most popular programming languages for machine learning due to its simplicity and the availability of powerful libraries and frameworks. Some of the most commonly used libraries for implementing machine learning in Python include:

- **scikit-learn**: A library for classical machine learning algorithms, including classification, regression, clustering, and dimensionality reduction.
- **TensorFlow**: An open-source deep learning framework developed by Google, useful for building and training neural networks.
- **Keras**: A high-level neural networks API, often used in conjunction with TensorFlow, that makes it easier to design and train deep learning models.
- **PyTorch**: Another deep learning framework, developed by Facebook, known for its flexibility and dynamic computational graphs.

In robotics, Python can be used for:

1. **Training Models**: Python libraries such as TensorFlow or scikit-learn can be used to train models on datasets, enabling robots to recognize patterns or make predictions.
2. **Data Preprocessing**: Data preparation (such as resizing images, normalizing values, or converting categorical data into numerical format) is essential in machine learning, and Python's libraries like NumPy and Pandas make this task easier.

3. **Deploying Models**: After training a model, Python can be used to integrate it into the robot's control system, enabling it to make real-time predictions or decisions based on sensor inputs.

Example: Using Python to Train a Model for Object Recognition

Let's create a simple object recognition system using a **Convolutional Neural Network (CNN)**, which is a deep learning algorithm commonly used for image recognition tasks. We will use the **TensorFlow** library to train the model on a popular dataset, **CIFAR-10**, which contains 60,000 images of 10 different classes (such as cats, dogs, cars, etc.).

Step 1: Installing Required Libraries

If you haven't already installed TensorFlow, you can do so using pip:

```bash
```

```
pip install tensorflow
```

Step 2: Loading and Preparing the Dataset

The CIFAR-10 dataset is available directly in TensorFlow, so we can load it using the built-in functions. We will also preprocess the data to normalize the pixel values for better training performance.

python

```
import tensorflow as tf
from tensorflow.keras import datasets, layers, models

# Load CIFAR-10 dataset
(x_train, y_train), (x_test, y_test) = datasets.cifar10.load_data()

# Normalize the pixel values to be between 0 and 1
x_train, x_test = x_train / 255.0, x_test / 255.0

# Print the shape of the training data
print("Training data shape:", x_train.shape)
```

Step 3: Building the CNN Model

We will build a simple CNN with three convolutional layers followed by dense layers for classification.

python

```python
# Build the CNN model
model = models.Sequential([
    layers.Conv2D(32, (3, 3), activation='relu',
input_shape=(32, 32, 3)),  # Convolutional layer
1
    layers.MaxPooling2D((2, 2)),  # Pooling layer
1
    layers.Conv2D(64,          (3,          3),
activation='relu'),  # Convolutional layer 2
    layers.MaxPooling2D((2, 2)),  # Pooling layer
2
    layers.Conv2D(64,          (3,          3),
activation='relu'),  # Convolutional layer 3
    layers.Flatten(),  # Flatten the data for the
dense layers
    layers.Dense(64, activation='relu'),     #
Dense layer
    layers.Dense(10, activation='softmax')    #
Output layer (10 classes)
])

# Compile the model
model.compile(optimizer='adam',

loss='sparse_categorical_crossentropy',
              metrics=['accuracy'])
```

Explanation:

- **Convolutional Layers**: These layers learn the features of the image (like edges, textures, and patterns). We use ReLU (Rectified Linear Unit) as the activation function for non-linearity.
- **Max Pooling Layers**: These layers reduce the spatial dimensions (height and width) of the image, helping to reduce computation and prevent overfitting.
- **Dense Layers**: These layers connect every neuron in the previous layer to every neuron in the current layer. The last dense layer has 10 output neurons (for the 10 classes).
- **Softmax Activation**: The softmax function outputs probabilities for each of the 10 classes.

Step 4: Training the Model

Now we'll train the model on the CIFAR-10 dataset.

python

```
# Train the model
model.fit(x_train, y_train, epochs=10)

# Evaluate the model on the test set
test_loss, test_acc = model.evaluate(x_test,
y_test, verbose=2)

print(f"Test accuracy: {test_acc}")
```

Explanation:

- The `model.fit()` function trains the model on the training data for 10 epochs.
- The `model.evaluate()` function evaluates the trained model on the test data and returns the loss and accuracy.

Step 5: Making Predictions

Once the model is trained, we can use it to make predictions on new images.

python

```
# Make a prediction on the test set
predictions = model.predict(x_test)

# Display the predicted class for the first image
in the test set
print(f"Predicted class: {predictions[0]}")
```

Expected Output: The model will output a vector of probabilities, one for each of the 10 classes. The class with the highest probability is the predicted label.

Conclusion

In this chapter, we introduced machine learning concepts and how Python, combined with libraries like TensorFlow, can be used to implement machine learning for robotics. We demonstrated how to train a Convolutional Neural Network (CNN) for object recognition using the CIFAR-10 dataset. This example illustrates the power of deep learning techniques in enabling robots to recognize objects and make intelligent decisions based on visual input.

Machine learning in robotics opens up new possibilities for autonomous decision-making, object manipulation, and more. By using Python and machine learning libraries, you can integrate advanced vision-based capabilities into your robotic systems, making them smarter and more capable of interacting with the environment.

CHAPTER 12

PATH PLANNING FOR ROBOTS

Introduction to Path Planning and Its Challenges

Path planning is a fundamental concept in robotics, enabling a robot to move from a starting point to a goal in an optimal way, often while avoiding obstacles. It is a critical component of autonomous robots, including those used for navigation, delivery, and exploration.

Challenges in Path Planning:

1. **Dynamic Environments**: In real-world scenarios, obstacles can change over time (e.g., moving objects, people, or environmental changes). Path planning needs to account for these dynamic changes and replan paths when necessary.

2. **Multiple Obstacles**: A robot must navigate through environments with varying complexity, such as narrow paths, irregular shapes, and multiple obstacles.

3. **Optimality**: The path planning algorithm should not only find a valid path but also try to optimize it in terms of cost,

time, or energy consumption. In many cases, the shortest or fastest path is desired.

4. **Real-Time Constraints**: Robots often need to plan and adjust paths in real-time, especially in scenarios like autonomous vehicles or drones where speed is essential for safety and performance.

Types of Path Planning:

- **Global Path Planning**: The robot plans a path from start to goal based on a full map of the environment. This is useful for static environments where the map is known in advance.

- **Local Path Planning**: The robot plans its path incrementally based on real-time sensor data. This is essential in dynamic environments or when the robot does not have access to a full map.

- **Replanning**: The robot continuously adjusts its path in response to environmental changes, often using feedback from sensors like cameras or LiDAR.

Basic Algorithms for Path Planning: A and Dijkstra's Algorithm*

Two of the most popular algorithms for path planning are **A*** and **Dijkstra's Algorithm**. Both algorithms help robots find the shortest path in a grid or graph-based environment, but they have some key differences in how they operate.

1. Dijkstra's Algorithm:

- Dijkstra's algorithm is a graph traversal algorithm that finds the shortest path from a starting point to all other points in a graph. It guarantees the shortest path by exploring all possible paths and choosing the one with the smallest cost.
- **Steps**:
    1. Initialize the distance of the start node to zero and all other nodes to infinity.
    2. Mark the current node as visited, then explore its neighbors.
    3. Update the distance of each neighbor.
    4. Repeat the process for the unvisited node with the smallest distance until the goal is reached.

Advantages:

- Guarantees the shortest path.
- Works well for both weighted and unweighted graphs.

Disadvantages:

- Can be slower compared to A* as it explores all possible paths without considering a heuristic.

2. A Algorithm*:

- A* is an extension of Dijkstra's algorithm that uses a heuristic to improve search efficiency. The heuristic guides the algorithm towards the goal, making it faster and more efficient than Dijkstra's in many cases.
- **Steps**:
    1. Similar to Dijkstra's, A* initializes the start node with zero distance and explores its neighbors.
    2. A* calculates the total cost for each node, which is the sum of the distance from the start and the estimated distance to the goal (heuristic).
    3. The algorithm chooses the node with the smallest total cost and continues the search.
    4. The search terminates when the goal is reached.

Advantages:

- More efficient than Dijkstra's because it uses a heuristic to prioritize nodes that are more likely to lead to the goal.
- Faster in practice for many types of problems, especially in large environments.

Disadvantages:

- The performance of A* depends heavily on the quality of the heuristic function.

- In some cases, A* may not find the optimal path if the heuristic is not admissible (i.e., it overestimates the cost).

Example: Using Python to Implement Pathfinding for a Robot

In this example, we will implement the **A*** algorithm for pathfinding in a simple grid-based environment using Python. The grid will consist of open spaces and obstacles, and the robot will need to find the shortest path from a start point to a goal point, avoiding obstacles.

Step 1: Define the Grid and Obstacles

Let's first define the grid and set up obstacles. In a grid, each cell can either be open or occupied by an obstacle.

python

```
import heapq

# Define the grid (0 is open, 1 is obstacle)
grid = [
    [0, 0, 0, 0, 0],
    [0, 1, 1, 0, 0],
    [0, 1, 0, 1, 0],
    [0, 0, 0, 0, 0],
    [0, 0, 0, 1, 0]
```

```
]


# Define start and goal positions
start = (0, 0)   # Starting point (row, col)
goal = (4, 4)    # Goal point (row, col)
```

*Step 2: A Algorithm Implementation**

Now, let's implement the A* algorithm to find the shortest path.

python

```
def heuristic(a, b):
    # Using Manhattan distance as the heuristic
    return abs(a[0] - b[0]) + abs(a[1] - b[1])

def a_star(grid, start, goal):
    # Directions (up, down, left, right)
    directions = [(0, 1), (1, 0), (0, -1), (-1, 0)]

    # Priority queue to store nodes to explore
    open_list = []
    heapq.heappush(open_list,        (0        +
heuristic(start, goal), 0, start))   # (f_score,
g_score, position)

    # Dictionary to store the best path
```

```python
came_from = {}
g_score = {start: 0}

while open_list:
    _,      current_g_score,      current    =
heapq.heappop(open_list)

    # If the goal is reached, reconstruct the
path
    if current == goal:
        path = []
        while current in came_from:
            path.append(current)
            current = came_from[current]
        path.append(start)
        return path[::-1]  # Return reversed
path

    # Explore neighbors
    for direction in directions:
        neighbor    =    (current[0]    +
direction[0], current[1] + direction[1])
        if 0 <= neighbor[0] < len(grid) and
0   <=   neighbor[1]   <   len(grid[0])   and
grid[neighbor[0]][neighbor[1]] == 0:
            tentative_g_score              =
current_g_score + 1
```

```
                if neighbor not in g_score or
tentative_g_score < g_score[neighbor]:
                    came_from[neighbor]        =
current
                    g_score[neighbor]          =
tentative_g_score
                    f_score = tentative_g_score
+ heuristic(neighbor, goal)
                    heapq.heappush(open_list,
(f_score, tentative_g_score, neighbor))

    return None  # No path found


# Run A* algorithm
path = a_star(grid, start, goal)

# Output the result
if path:
    print("Path found:", path)
else:
    print("No path found.")
```

Explanation of the Code:

1. **Heuristic Function**: We use the Manhattan distance (the sum of the absolute differences in x and y coordinates) as the heuristic to guide the A* search.

2. **A* Algorithm**:

- We maintain an open list (priority queue) that stores nodes to explore, sorted by their `f_score` (the sum of the cost so far and the heuristic).
- We keep track of the **g_score** (the cost from the start node to the current node) and use it to determine whether a better path has been found to a particular node.
- The algorithm explores the neighbors of the current node, updating their g-scores and calculating their f-scores. If a better path is found, it updates the path information (`came_from`).
- The search continues until the goal node is reached or there are no more nodes to explore.

Step 3: Output

The output will show the path found by the A* algorithm, if one exists. For example:

pgsql

```
Path found: [(0, 0), (0, 1), (1, 1), (1, 2), (2,
2), (3, 2), (4, 2), (4, 3), (4, 4)]
```

Conclusion

In this chapter, we explored the concept of **path planning** for robots, including the challenges robots face in navigating environments. We discussed two popular algorithms for pathfinding: **Dijkstra's Algorithm** and **A***, and implemented the **A*** algorithm in Python for finding the shortest path in a grid-based environment.

Path planning is crucial in robotics, allowing robots to navigate efficiently and autonomously. Whether for obstacle avoidance, navigation in dynamic environments, or robotic arms, path planning algorithms like A* can help robots make intelligent decisions and move from one point to another safely and optimally.

CHAPTER 13

LOCALIZATION AND MAPPING

What is Robot Localization and Mapping?

Robot localization is the process by which a robot determines its position and orientation within a given environment. This is essential for any autonomous robot, as it needs to know where it is to navigate and interact with its surroundings effectively. Localization involves estimating the robot's position relative to a known map or relative to a series of sensors within the environment.

Robot mapping is the process of creating a representation of the environment, typically in the form of a map. This allows a robot to understand its surroundings and plan paths more efficiently. Mapping involves gathering data from sensors such as lasers, cameras, and depth sensors, and using that data to build a model of the environment.

Together, **localization and mapping** are often referred to as **SLAM (Simultaneous Localization and Mapping)**. In SLAM, the robot must both estimate its position while simultaneously building a map of the environment. SLAM is crucial for robots that need to navigate autonomously in unknown or dynamic environments without relying on preexisting maps.

Using Python to Implement Simultaneous Localization and Mapping (SLAM)

SLAM is a complex process, but it can be broken down into several key components:

1. **Sensor Data Collection**: Robots use various sensors to collect data about their environment, such as **LiDAR** (Light Detection and Ranging), **cameras**, or **ultrasonic sensors**.

2. **Feature Extraction**: From the sensor data, robots extract features such as points, lines, or landmarks that will help build the map.

3. **Pose Estimation**: The robot estimates its position and orientation (pose) in the environment based on its sensor data.

4. **Map Creation**: Using the sensor data and pose information, the robot creates a map of its environment, updating it as it moves.

5. **Loop Closure**: When the robot revisits a previously mapped area, it can "close the loop" by recognizing the environment, reducing the accumulated error in its position estimate.

Python, along with libraries like **OpenCV**, **ROS (Robot Operating System)**, and **PySLAM**, can be used to implement SLAM algorithms.

Common SLAM algorithms include:

- **Extended Kalman Filter (EKF) SLAM**: An approach that uses an extended Kalman filter to estimate both the robot's position and the map.
- **FastSLAM**: A particle filter-based method that handles large-scale environments.
- **ORB-SLAM**: A feature-based SLAM approach that uses visual information to build a map.

While implementing full SLAM algorithms in Python can be complex, it's possible to build simple versions of SLAM using libraries like **OpenCV** for vision-based SLAM or **ROS** for integrating sensors and localization algorithms.

Example: Using Python to Create a Basic Map Using Sensor Data

In this example, we will implement a simple **grid-based mapping** approach where a robot uses a sensor (such as an ultrasonic sensor or a simulated LiDAR) to create a basic map of its environment. We'll simulate the robot's movement and use sensor data to build a 2D occupancy grid map.

Step 1: Installing Required Libraries

For this example, we will use the **NumPy** and **matplotlib** libraries to create and visualize the map.

```bash
pip install numpy matplotlib
```

Step 2: Defining the Environment and Robot Movement

Let's define a simple environment and simulate the robot's movement while collecting sensor data. The robot will move around a grid and detect obstacles in its environment.

```python
import numpy as np
import matplotlib.pyplot as plt
```

```python
# Define the grid size and environment (0 = free
space, 1 = obstacle)
grid_size = 10  # 10x10 grid
environment = np.zeros((grid_size, grid_size))  #
Free space
environment[3:6, 3:6] = 1  # An obstacle (a 3x3
block)

# Define the robot's starting position
robot_position = [0, 0]

# Define the map (initially empty)
robot_map = np.zeros((grid_size, grid_size))

# Define the sensor range (in grid units)
sensor_range = 2

# Function to simulate robot sensor (detect
obstacles within range)
def get_sensor_data(position, range):
    x, y = position
    sensor_data = []

    for dx in range(-range, range + 1):
        for dy in range(-range, range + 1):
            if 0 <= x + dx < grid_size and 0 <=
y + dy < grid_size:
```

```python
            sensor_data.append((x + dx, y + dy))

    return sensor_data

# Function to update the map based on sensor data
def update_map(sensor_data, map_grid):
    for (x, y) in sensor_data:
        map_grid[x, y] = 1  # Mark the grid cell as occupied (detected by sensor)

# Simulate robot movement and map updates
for step in range(5):
    print(f"Robot position: {robot_position}")

    # Get sensor data from the current position
    sensor_data                     = get_sensor_data(robot_position, sensor_range)

    # Update the robot's map with the detected sensor data
    update_map(sensor_data, robot_map)

    # Simulate robot movement (moving right and down)
    robot_position[0] += 1
    robot_position[1] += 1

# Visualize the robot's map
```

```
plt.imshow(robot_map,                    cmap='gray',
interpolation='nearest')
plt.title("Robot Map (Occupancy Grid)")
plt.colorbar()
plt.show()
```

Explanation of the Code:

1. **Grid Setup**: We create a 10x10 grid representing the environment. The environment contains an obstacle (a 3x3 block) in the center.

2. **Robot Position**: The robot starts at position (0, 0).

3. **Sensor Data Simulation**: The `get_sensor_data` function simulates the robot's sensor. The robot scans a range of cells around it to detect obstacles. The range is defined as `sensor_range`.

4. **Map Update**: The `update_map` function marks the detected cells in the `robot_map`. As the robot moves, its sensor readings help build a map of the environment.

5. **Robot Movement**: The robot moves diagonally across the grid by updating its position in each step.

6. **Visualization**: After simulating the robot's movement and mapping, we use `matplotlib` to visualize the occupancy grid map, where white cells represent detected obstacles, and black cells represent free space.

Step 3: Expected Output

The output will be a visual representation of the robot's map. Initially, the robot starts at the top-left corner and detects obstacles in its environment based on its sensor range. After moving a few steps, the map will show the areas the robot has explored, with obstacles marked.

Conclusion

In this chapter, we discussed **robot localization and mapping**—two essential aspects of enabling a robot to navigate and understand its environment. We introduced the concept of **Simultaneous Localization and Mapping (SLAM)**, which allows robots to build maps while simultaneously determining their location.

We implemented a simple example using Python to simulate a robot's movement and sensor data collection, resulting in an occupancy grid map of its environment. This basic map-building process lays the foundation for more advanced SLAM algorithms that can be applied to real-world robotic applications.

For more sophisticated implementations, robots often rely on advanced sensors (such as LiDAR or cameras), and algorithms like **EKF-SLAM**, **FastSLAM**, or **ORB-SLAM** are used to handle larger, more complex environments. By combining these techniques with Python and libraries like **OpenCV**, **ROS**, and **PySLAM**, robots can navigate autonomously and interact with their surroundings intelligently.

CHAPTER 14

AUTONOMOUS NAVIGATION

Introduction to Autonomous Navigation and Its Importance

Autonomous navigation refers to a robot's ability to navigate through an environment without human intervention. The goal is for the robot to plan its path, avoid obstacles, and reach its destination safely and efficiently. Autonomous navigation is essential in a wide range of robotic applications, such as:

- **Self-driving cars**: Navigating through traffic and obstacles while following traffic rules.
- **Robotic vacuum cleaners**: Moving around a home while avoiding furniture and other obstacles.
- **Delivery robots**: Navigating through warehouses or outdoor environments to deliver goods.
- **Drones**: Flying autonomously in airspace, avoiding obstacles, and reaching predefined destinations.

Autonomous navigation relies on a combination of:

1. **Sensors** (e.g., cameras, LiDAR, sonar) to perceive the environment.
2. **Path planning algorithms** (e.g., A*, Dijkstra's) to find the optimal path.
3. **Control algorithms** (e.g., PID control) to adjust the robot's movement in real-time.

The importance of autonomous navigation in robotics cannot be overstated, as it enables robots to perform tasks that would be too complex, repetitive, or dangerous for humans. It also opens up possibilities for robots to operate in unknown or changing environments without human supervision.

Using Python to Control Autonomous Movement

Python is widely used to control robotic movement due to its simplicity and versatility. By leveraging libraries such as **RPi.GPIO** for hardware control, **OpenCV** for vision-based navigation, and **scikit-learn** or **TensorFlow** for machine learning-based navigation, Python provides a powerful platform for developing autonomous robots.

In autonomous navigation, the following components are typically involved:

1. **Sensors for perception**: Cameras, LiDAR, and ultrasonic sensors provide the robot with real-time environmental data.

2. **Path planning**: Algorithms like **A*** and **Dijkstra's** help the robot decide the best route to reach its destination.

3. **Obstacle avoidance**: Using real-time sensor data, the robot needs to avoid obstacles in its path.

4. **Control systems**: The robot needs to execute its planned path by adjusting its speed and direction. Common control methods include **PID control** (Proportional-Integral-Derivative) to maintain steady movement.

We will explore how Python can be used to combine sensor data and path planning to control autonomous movement.

Real-World Example: Programming a Robot to Navigate Around Obstacles

In this example, we will simulate a robot navigating through a simple environment, avoiding obstacles using ultrasonic sensors. We'll use Python to control the robot's movement by reading sensor data, detecting obstacles, and adjusting the robot's path accordingly.

Step 1: Setting Up the Environment

We will simulate the robot's movement in a 2D environment using basic Python code. In a real-world scenario, the robot would use sensors like ultrasonic distance sensors or LiDAR to detect obstacles.

Let's assume the robot has two basic functions:

- **Move Forward**: The robot moves straight ahead.
- **Turn**: The robot turns to avoid obstacles when detected.

The robot will use an **ultrasonic sensor** (simulated here as a simple distance check) to detect obstacles in front of it.

Step 2: Simulating Obstacle Detection and Avoidance

We will create a basic simulation using Python, where the robot checks its surroundings, detects obstacles, and avoids them.

```python
import random
import time

# Define the robot's grid size
grid_size = 10
robot_position = [0, 0]  # Start at the top-left
corner
```

```python
# Define a simple obstacle (1 represents an
obstacle, 0 represents free space)
environment = [[0 for _ in range(grid_size)] for
_ in range(grid_size)]
# Add some random obstacles
for _ in range(10):
    x = random.randint(0, grid_size - 1)
    y = random.randint(0, grid_size - 1)
    environment[x][y] = 1


# Simulated ultrasonic sensor function to check
distance
def get_distance():
    # Return a random "distance" value from 1 to
3 (representing obstacles at different ranges)
    return random.randint(1, 3)


# Simulated robot movement functions
def move_forward():
    # Check if there's an obstacle ahead
    distance = get_distance()
    print(f"Distance to obstacle: {distance}
units")

    if distance < 2:
        print("Obstacle detected! Turning...")
        turn_away()
    else:
```

```
    print("Moving forward...")
    robot_position[0] += 1  # Move forward in
the x-direction


def turn_away():
    # Turn the robot to avoid obstacle (change
direction)
    print("Turning left...")
    robot_position[1] += 1  # Move in the y-
direction instead


def show_environment():
    # Display the environment grid with the
robot's current position
    grid = [["." for _ in range(grid_size)] for
_ in range(grid_size)]
    x, y = robot_position
    grid[x][y] = "R"  # Mark the robot's position
with 'R'
    for row in grid:
        print(" ".join(row))


# Simulate robot navigating the environment
for _ in range(15):  # Simulate 15 steps
    show_environment()
    move_forward()
    time.sleep(1)  # Pause for a second before
moving again
    print()
```

Explanation:

1. **Environment Setup**: The environment is a 10x10 grid, with random obstacles represented by 1 (obstacle) and 0 (empty space). The robot starts at position (0, 0).

2. **Sensor Simulation**: The `get_distance()` function simulates the behavior of an ultrasonic sensor. It returns a random "distance" value representing the distance to an obstacle.

3. **Movement Functions**:
   - `move_forward()` checks the distance ahead and determines whether to move forward or turn.
   - `turn_away()` is called if an obstacle is detected within a range of 1 or 2 units, simulating a turn to avoid the obstacle.

4. **Grid Display**: The `show_environment()` function prints the current state of the robot's environment, showing where the robot (R) is located in the grid.

5. **Simulation Loop**: The loop simulates the robot moving for 15 steps. Each step checks the sensor data and makes decisions based on the distance to the nearest obstacle.

Step 3: Expected Output

The output will display the robot's position in the grid and the actions taken based on the sensor data. Here's an example output:

```vbnet
. . . . . . . . . .
R . . . . . . . . .
Distance to obstacle: 2 units
Moving forward...

. . . . . . . . . .
. R . . . . . . . .
Distance to obstacle: 1 unit
Obstacle detected! Turning...

. . . . . . . . . .
. R . . . . . . . .
Distance to obstacle: 3 units
Moving forward...
```

The robot will move forward when there's no obstacle in front of it and will turn when an obstacle is detected.

Conclusion

In this chapter, we explored **autonomous navigation** and its significance in robotics. We learned how Python can be used to control a robot's movement, making decisions based on sensor data and obstacle detection. By combining sensor inputs, path planning, and control algorithms, robots can navigate autonomously, avoiding obstacles and adjusting their path in real-time.

Through the example of programming a robot to navigate around obstacles, we illustrated the basics of autonomous movement, showing how a simple approach can simulate obstacle detection and avoidance. In real-world applications, this can be extended by incorporating more advanced sensors (like LiDAR, cameras, or depth sensors) and more complex algorithms (such as **PID control**, **SLAM**, and **path planning algorithms**) to enable more sophisticated autonomous navigation.

CHAPTER 15

INTEGRATING MACHINE VISION WITH ROBOTICS

Combining Machine Vision with Motion Control

In robotics, **machine vision** and **motion control** are two key components that enable robots to interact with their environment autonomously. By combining these technologies, robots can perform complex tasks such as object detection, identification, and manipulation.

- **Machine Vision**: Provides robots with the ability to "see" the environment using cameras, sensors, and image processing algorithms. The robot uses vision to perceive objects, detect obstacles, recognize patterns, and understand its surroundings.
- **Motion Control**: Allows the robot to move or manipulate objects based on the information provided by the vision system. This could involve adjusting the robot's position, orientation, or even applying force to pick up, move, or place objects.

When machine vision is integrated with motion control, the robot can make decisions based on its visual input and adjust its movements accordingly. For example, it can locate and pick up an object, avoiding obstacles along the way.

Real-World Example: Programming a Robot to Pick Up Objects Using Vision

In this example, we will simulate a simple robotic system that uses machine vision to identify and pick up objects. The robot will use a **camera** to locate an object, process the image to identify the object's position, and then move to that position to pick up the object using motion control.

For simplicity, we will use a **simulated robot** and **OpenCV** for object detection. The robot will detect a simple object in the camera's view and "move" towards it, simulating the process of picking it up. The motion control will be handled by simple functions to move the robot in a 2D environment.

Step 1: Setting Up the Environment

Let's create a simple environment with a robot and an object. We will simulate the robot's camera capturing an image of the environment and processing it to detect the object.

```python
python

import numpy as np
import cv2
import random
import time

# Define the environment size (grid size)
grid_size = 10
environment = np.zeros((grid_size, grid_size,
3), dtype=np.uint8)  # Empty grid

# Define robot and object positions
robot_position = [0, 0]
object_position = [random.randint(1, grid_size -
1), random.randint(1, grid_size - 1)]

# Draw the object in the environment (e.g., red
square represents the object)
environment[object_position[0],
object_position[1]] = [0, 0, 255]  # Red object

# Function to display the environment
def show_environment():
    # Create a blank white grid
```

```python
    grid = np.ones((grid_size, grid_size, 3),
dtype=np.uint8) * 255
    x, y = robot_position
    grid[x, y] = [0, 255, 0]  # Green robot

    # Place the object in the grid
    grid[object_position[0], object_position[1]]
= [0, 0, 255]  # Red object

    # Show the environment
    cv2.imshow('Robot Environment', grid)
    cv2.waitKey(1)

# Function to simulate robot camera (detect the
object)
def detect_object():
    # Check if the robot's position matches the
object position
    if robot_position == object_position:
        print("Object detected at position:",
object_position)
        return True
    return False

# Function to move robot towards the object
def move_towards_object():
    global robot_position
    x, y = robot_position
    object_x, object_y = object_position
```

```python
    # Move robot towards the object (simple
decision logic)
    if x < object_x:
        x += 1
    elif x > object_x:
        x -= 1

    if y < object_y:
        y += 1
    elif y > object_y:
        y -= 1

    robot_position = [x, y]
    print(f"Moving          to          position:
{robot_position}")
    time.sleep(0.5)

# Simulate the process
for step in range(20):   # Simulate 20 steps
    show_environment()  # Display the environment

    if detect_object():   # Check if object is
detected
        print("Object  is  now  within  range.
Picking up the object.")
        break
```

```
    move_towards_object()    # Move towards the
object
    time.sleep(1)

cv2.destroyAllWindows()
```

Explanation of the Code:

1. **Environment Setup**: We create a 10x10 grid as the robot's environment using NumPy, where each grid cell represents a part of the environment. The robot and the object are placed in random locations within the grid.

2. **Object Detection**: The `detect_object()` function checks if the robot's position matches the object's position. If they coincide, the robot "detects" the object.

3. **Moving Towards the Object**: The `move_towards_object()` function adjusts the robot's position by one unit at each step, moving towards the object.

4. **Visualization**: The `show_environment()` function displays the current environment using OpenCV, showing the robot as a green square and the object as a red square.

5. **Simulation Loop**: The robot moves towards the object in steps, and once it reaches the object, it simulates the "picking up" of the object.

Step 2: Expected Output

During the simulation, the robot will move towards the object, and once it reaches the object, the message "Object detected at position" will be printed, simulating the process of the robot picking up the object.

Integrating Machine Vision and Motion Control

In real-world applications, machine vision and motion control are integrated in several steps:

1. **Vision-Based Object Detection**: The robot uses cameras or vision sensors to detect objects in its environment. For example, using OpenCV to process images and identify key features (such as edges, colors, or shapes).

2. **Processing and Localization**: The robot processes the captured images to determine the object's position in the 3D world (localization). This can involve algorithms like **SLAM** or simple 2D object detection.

3. **Motion Control**: Based on the detected object position, the robot adjusts its movement using algorithms like **PID** control or **inverse kinematics** for robotic arms. The robot plans its path toward the object and adjusts its position to "pick it up."

4. **Manipulation**: Once the robot reaches the object, it uses motion control to grasp or manipulate the object, based on the vision system's feedback.

In real-world systems, the integration of machine vision and motion control is often done using more sophisticated algorithms and control loops, enabling robots to perform tasks such as:

- **Object sorting and picking**: Robots can identify, pick, and place objects in industrial settings (e.g., warehouse automation).
- **Human-robot interaction**: Robots can recognize and respond to human gestures or commands.
- **Autonomous vehicles**: Self-driving cars use a combination of cameras, LiDAR, and motion control to navigate roads, detect pedestrians, and avoid collisions.

Conclusion

In this chapter, we explored how to integrate **machine vision** with **motion control** in robotics. We demonstrated how Python and OpenCV can be used for basic object detection and how this can be combined with simple motion control algorithms to program a robot to pick up objects.

The integration of machine vision with motion control allows robots to perform sophisticated tasks autonomously, using real-time visual feedback to navigate, interact with objects, and make decisions. This combination is critical in applications such as industrial automation, autonomous vehicles, and personal assistant robots.

As you move forward with your own robotic projects, combining vision and motion control will be key to developing intelligent robots capable of complex tasks in dynamic environments.

CHAPTER 16

ROBOT ARM CONTROL WITH PYTHON

Introduction to Robotic Arm Control

A **robotic arm** is a type of robot that is designed to perform tasks that typically require human hands. It is composed of multiple joints (also called **degrees of freedom**, or **DOF**) and links that allow it to move in various directions. Robotic arms are widely used in industries like manufacturing, assembly, packaging, and even surgery. They are also used in research and education, as well as in service robots for tasks like picking and placing objects.

Controlling a robotic arm involves managing the movement of its joints and end-effector (the part that interacts with objects, such as a gripper or tool). This requires precise control over each joint's position, speed, and orientation to complete tasks like picking up, moving, and releasing objects.

Key concepts in robotic arm control include:

1. **Degrees of Freedom (DOF)**: Refers to the number of independent movements a robot arm can make. A typical robotic arm might have 5 or 6 DOF, meaning it can move in 5 or 6 independent directions.

2. **Inverse Kinematics**: The process of calculating the necessary joint angles or positions to reach a desired position of the end-effector.

3. **Forward Kinematics**: The calculation of the end-effector's position and orientation based on known joint angles or positions.

4. **Motion Control**: Ensuring smooth and precise movement of the arm, including speed control, position control, and feedback control.

Python is commonly used to control robotic arms because it offers simplicity and ease of integration with hardware. Using libraries such as **RPi.GPIO**, **pySerial**, or higher-level frameworks like **ROS (Robot Operating System)**, Python allows us to control robotic arms, implement inverse kinematics, and develop control algorithms.

Using Python to Control the Degrees of Freedom in a Robot Arm

A robotic arm typically consists of several segments connected by joints. These joints are actuated by motors or servos, which allow the arm to move in specific directions. Each joint's position can be controlled by adjusting its angle, and the arm's overall position is determined by the combination of these joint movements.

In this section, we will use Python to control a **simulated robotic arm**. The arm will have **3 degrees of freedom (DOF)**: a shoulder joint, an elbow joint, and a wrist joint. We will write Python code to control the angles of each joint and move the arm in a 2D plane.

We'll assume that the arm uses **servo motors** to control the joint angles. Servo motors are common in robotic arms and can be controlled by sending a PWM (Pulse Width Modulation) signal.

For simplicity, we will not connect to actual hardware but simulate the control logic for educational purposes.

Example: Controlling a Robot Arm to Perform Tasks Like Grabbing and Releasing

In this example, we'll simulate controlling the robotic arm's joint angles and using it to perform tasks like grabbing and releasing objects.

Step 1: Defining the Arm's Kinematics

We'll define the arm with 3 joints (shoulder, elbow, and wrist). The lengths of the arm segments will be set as constants, and the angles of the joints will be used to compute the end-effector's position.

Kinematic equations for a 2D robotic arm:

- ```
  x = l1 * cos(θ1) + l2 * cos(θ1 + θ2)
  ```
- ```
  y = l1 * sin(θ1) + l2 * sin(θ1 + θ2)
  ```

Where:

- `l1` and `l2` are the lengths of the arm segments (shoulder to elbow, elbow to wrist).
- `θ1` and `θ2` are the angles of the shoulder and elbow joints, respectively.

Step 2: Simulating the Arm's Motion

144

```python
python

import numpy as np
import matplotlib.pyplot as plt

# Arm parameters
l1 = 5    # Length of the first arm segment
(shoulder to elbow)
l2 = 4  # Length of the second arm segment (elbow
to wrist)

# Function to calculate the end-effector position
using forward kinematics
def forward_kinematics(theta1, theta2):
    x = l1 * np.cos(np.radians(theta1)) + l2 *
np.cos(np.radians(theta1 + theta2))
    y = l1 * np.sin(np.radians(theta1)) + l2 *
np.sin(np.radians(theta1 + theta2))
    return x, y

# Function to plot the robot arm
def plot_arm(theta1, theta2):
    x1, y1 = forward_kinematics(theta1, 0)    #
Position of the elbow
    x2, y2 = forward_kinematics(theta1, theta2)
# Position of the wrist (end-effector)

    # Plot the robot arm
```

```python
    plt.plot([0,     x1],     [0,     y1],     'b',
label="Shoulder to Elbow")
    plt.plot([x1,     x2],     [y1,     y2],     'r',
label="Elbow to Wrist")
    plt.scatter([0,   x1,   x2],   [0,   y1,   y2],
color="black")   # Mark the joints
    plt.text(0,     0,     "Start",     fontsize=12,
ha='right')
    plt.text(x1,   y1,   "Elbow",   fontsize=12,
ha='right')
    plt.text(x2,   y2,   "Wrist",   fontsize=12,
ha='right')

    plt.xlim(-10, 10)
    plt.ylim(-10, 10)
    plt.gca().set_aspect('equal',
adjustable='box')
    plt.legend()
    plt.show()

# Simulating robot arm movement
theta1 = 45   # Shoulder angle
theta2 = 30   # Elbow angle

# Plot arm's initial position
plot_arm(theta1, theta2)

# Simulate moving the arm by changing the angles
theta1 += 10   # Move shoulder joint
```

```
theta2 += 15   # Move elbow joint

# Plot new arm position
plot_arm(theta1, theta2)
```

Explanation:

1. **Forward Kinematics**: The `forward_kinematics()` function calculates the x and y positions of the end-effector (wrist) using the angles of the shoulder and elbow joints. This is based on the kinematic equations.

2. **Arm Simulation**: The `plot_arm()` function visualizes the arm in 2D by plotting the segments and joints. It also labels the joints and updates the arm's position when the angles change.

3. **Simulation**: Initially, the shoulder (`theta1`) and elbow (`theta2`) angles are set to 45 and 30 degrees, respectively. After that, the angles are updated to simulate the arm's movement.

Step 3: Expected Output

The output will show a 2D plot of the robotic arm in its initial position and after moving. The robot arm's configuration will change based on the updated joint angles.

Real-World Application: Grabbing and Releasing Objects

In a real robotic arm, the task of grabbing and releasing objects involves a **gripper** at the end of the arm. The robot uses its machine vision system to detect the object's position, then moves the gripper to that position to pick up the object.

1. **Object Detection**: The robot uses cameras or vision sensors to detect the object and calculate its position.
2. **Gripper Control**: The robot arm moves the gripper to the object's position, using the inverse kinematics (IK) of the arm to calculate the necessary joint angles.
3. **Grabbing**: The robot's gripper closes around the object.
4. **Releasing**: The robot moves the object to a new location and opens the gripper to release it.

The control for grabbing and releasing involves both **motion control** (moving the arm) and **gripper control** (activating the gripper to pick up or release an object).

Conclusion

In this chapter, we explored **robotic arm control** using Python, focusing on controlling the degrees of freedom (DOF) of a robot arm. We implemented a simple **forward**

kinematics solution to simulate the movement of a 2D robotic arm and demonstrated how to control the angles of the shoulder and elbow joints to move the arm.

By combining **motion control** and **machine vision**, robots can perform complex tasks like grabbing and releasing objects autonomously. This chapter serves as a foundation for more advanced robotic arm control, including the use of **inverse kinematics**, **motion planning**, and **gripper control**, which are essential in real-world robotic applications.

CHAPTER 17

WORKING WITH ARDUINO AND RASPBERRY PI FOR ROBOTICS

Overview of Arduino and Raspberry Pi in Robotics

Both **Arduino** and **Raspberry Pi** are powerful and versatile platforms commonly used in robotics projects. While they each have different capabilities and use cases, they are both essential tools for building robots and other embedded systems.

Arduino:

- **What is Arduino?** Arduino is an open-source electronics platform based on easy-to-use hardware and software. It's widely used in robotics for controlling motors, sensors, and other components.
- **Why Arduino in Robotics?** Arduino excels in handling real-time control and low-level tasks, such as controlling sensors and actuators (e.g., motors, LEDs). It's great for small, low-power robotics applications where simple, low-latency control is required.

- **Capabilities**: Arduino boards, such as the **Arduino Uno**, contain microcontrollers with digital and analog I/O pins for connecting various sensors, actuators, and other electronics. The simplicity of Arduino's programming environment makes it ideal for prototyping and simple robotics systems.

Raspberry Pi:

- **What is Raspberry Pi?** Raspberry Pi is a single-board computer that runs a full operating system (usually **Raspberry Pi OS**) and offers higher processing power than Arduino. It's capable of handling more complex tasks such as image processing, communication, and running machine learning models.
- **Why Raspberry Pi in Robotics?** Raspberry Pi is often used in robotics for tasks that require greater processing power, such as **computer vision**, **network communication**, and **data processing**. It can interface with sensors and actuators through its GPIO pins, similar to Arduino, but it also supports advanced capabilities like Wi-Fi, Bluetooth, and HDMI video output.
- **Capabilities**: Raspberry Pi can run Python, making it a powerful platform for high-level control, while also having GPIO pins for interfacing with motors, sensors, and other hardware.

151

Arduino and Raspberry Pi Together:

- Many robotics projects combine **Arduino** and **Raspberry Pi**. The Raspberry Pi is used for higher-level tasks like image processing and networking, while the Arduino controls low-level tasks like motor control and sensor readings. They communicate via serial communication (e.g., USB or UART) to work together seamlessly.

Setting Up Python to Interface with Arduino and Raspberry Pi

To interface Python with Arduino and Raspberry Pi, we need to use different tools and libraries for each platform. Let's go over how to set up Python for both platforms.

1. Interfacing Python with Arduino:

- **Hardware**: Arduino board (e.g., Arduino Uno), USB cable to connect Arduino to your computer or Raspberry Pi.
- **Software**: Python library **pySerial** is commonly used to communicate with Arduino over serial.

Steps:

1. **Install pySerial**:

```bash
bash
```

```bash
pip install pyserial
```

2. **Upload an Arduino Sketch**: Write an Arduino program (sketch) that listens for commands via the serial port and controls motors, sensors, or LEDs. For example:

```cpp
cpp
```

```cpp
void setup() {
  Serial.begin(9600);    // Start serial
communication at 9600 baud
  pinMode(9, OUTPUT);   // Set pin 9 as an
output (for motor control)
}

void loop() {
  if (Serial.available() > 0) {
    char command = Serial.read();   // Read
the incoming byte
    if (command == '1') {
      digitalWrite(9, HIGH);   // Turn on
motor
    } else if (command == '0') {
      digitalWrite(9, LOW);   // Turn off
motor
    }
```

153

```
        }
    }
```

3. **Python Code for Communication**: Use Python to send commands to the Arduino.

```python
python

import serial
import time

# Setup serial communication (adjust port
and baud rate)
ser = serial.Serial('/dev/ttyUSB0', 9600)
# For Linux/Mac, check your device name
(e.g., /dev/ttyUSB0)
time.sleep(2)  # Give Arduino time to reset

# Send command to turn motor on
ser.write(b'1')

time.sleep(2)  # Wait for 2 seconds

# Send command to turn motor off
ser.write(b'0')

# Close the serial communication
ser.close()
```

2. Interfacing Python with Raspberry Pi:

- **Hardware**: Raspberry Pi with Raspberry Pi OS installed.
- **Software**: Raspberry Pi provides a built-in library called **RPi.GPIO** to control GPIO pins from Python.

Steps:

1. **Install RPi.GPIO**:

```bash
pip install RPi.GPIO
```

2. **Python Code for Controlling Motors**: This example controls a motor via a **motor driver** (e.g., L298N or L293D) connected to the GPIO pins of Raspberry Pi.

```python
import RPi.GPIO as GPIO
import time

# Setup GPIO mode
GPIO.setmode(GPIO.BCM)

# Define GPIO pins connected to the motor driver
```

155

```python
IN1 = 17
IN2 = 18
ENA = 27

# Set GPIO pins as output
GPIO.setup(IN1, GPIO.OUT)
GPIO.setup(IN2, GPIO.OUT)
GPIO.setup(ENA, GPIO.OUT)

# Enable the motor driver
GPIO.output(ENA, GPIO.HIGH)

# Turn motor on (forward direction)
GPIO.output(IN1, GPIO.HIGH)
GPIO.output(IN2, GPIO.LOW)

time.sleep(2)   # Motor runs for 2 seconds

# Turn motor off
GPIO.output(IN1, GPIO.LOW)
GPIO.output(IN2, GPIO.LOW)

# Clean up GPIO
GPIO.cleanup()
```

This example turns a motor on and off using a Raspberry Pi, controlling it via the GPIO pins. The motor driver (e.g., L298N) is used to provide enough current to the motor.

Example: Using Python to Control Motors via Raspberry Pi

In this section, we will walk through an example where the Raspberry Pi is used to control motors based on sensor input or commands. Suppose we have a robot with two motors controlled by the Raspberry Pi's GPIO pins. We will write a Python program to control the motors for simple movement, like moving forward, backward, and stopping.

Hardware Setup:

- Raspberry Pi connected to a motor driver (e.g., L298N).
- Two DC motors connected to the motor driver.

Python Code for Motor Control:

```python
python

import RPi.GPIO as GPIO
import time

# Setup GPIO pins
GPIO.setmode(GPIO.BCM)

# Motor driver pins (for two motors)
IN1 = 17
IN2 = 18
```

```
IN3 = 22
IN4 = 23
ENA = 24
ENB = 25

# Set pins as output
GPIO.setup(IN1, GPIO.OUT)
GPIO.setup(IN2, GPIO.OUT)
GPIO.setup(IN3, GPIO.OUT)
GPIO.setup(IN4, GPIO.OUT)
GPIO.setup(ENA, GPIO.OUT)
GPIO.setup(ENB, GPIO.OUT)

# Enable the motor driver
GPIO.output(ENA, GPIO.HIGH)
GPIO.output(ENB, GPIO.HIGH)

# Function to move forward
def move_forward():
    GPIO.output(IN1, GPIO.HIGH)
    GPIO.output(IN2, GPIO.LOW)
    GPIO.output(IN3, GPIO.HIGH)
    GPIO.output(IN4, GPIO.LOW)

# Function to move backward
def move_backward():
    GPIO.output(IN1, GPIO.LOW)
    GPIO.output(IN2, GPIO.HIGH)
    GPIO.output(IN3, GPIO.LOW)
```

```
    GPIO.output(IN4, GPIO.HIGH)

# Function to stop
def stop_movement():
    GPIO.output(IN1, GPIO.LOW)
    GPIO.output(IN2, GPIO.LOW)
    GPIO.output(IN3, GPIO.LOW)
    GPIO.output(IN4, GPIO.LOW)

# Example usage
move_forward()
time.sleep(2)  # Move forward for 2 seconds

move_backward()
time.sleep(2)  # Move backward for 2 seconds

stop_movement()

# Cleanup GPIO
GPIO.cleanup()
```

Explanation:

- **Motor Control**: The `move_forward()` function makes the motors rotate in the forward direction, and `move_backward()` makes them rotate in the opposite direction. The `stop_movement()` function stops the motors.

159

- **GPIO Pins**: We use the GPIO pins to control the motor driver, sending signals to control the direction of the motors.
- **Timing**: The robot moves forward and then backward for 2 seconds each, demonstrating basic movement control.

Conclusion

In this chapter, we explored how to interface **Python** with both **Arduino** and **Raspberry Pi** for robotics applications. We covered the basics of controlling motors with these platforms, with examples using **pySerial** for Arduino and **RPi.GPIO** for Raspberry Pi.

Arduino is well-suited for low-level control tasks, like reading sensors and driving motors, while **Raspberry Pi** is better for high-level processing, running complex algorithms, and controlling more advanced peripherals. When combined, they offer a powerful solution for building intelligent robots capable of performing a wide range of tasks.

Whether you are controlling simple movements or designing complex robotic systems, Python provides a flexible and powerful interface for both platforms, enabling you to prototype and implement robotic applications effectively.

CHAPTER 18

COLLABORATIVE ROBOTS
(COBOTS)

Introduction to Collaborative Robots: What Are They and Why Are
They Important?

Collaborative robots (cobots) are robots designed to work safely and efficiently alongside human operators in shared workspaces. Unlike traditional industrial robots, which operate in isolated environments due to safety concerns, cobots are designed with features that allow them to collaborate directly with humans. They can be used in tasks such as assembly, packaging, welding, and material handling.

Why Are Cobots Important?

1. **Safety and Flexibility**: Cobots are designed with advanced safety features like force sensors and collision detection, which allow them to work closely with humans without the need for physical

barriers. This flexibility enables them to adapt to various tasks and work environments.

2. **Improved Productivity**: By working alongside human workers, cobots can enhance productivity by taking over repetitive or physically demanding tasks, allowing human workers to focus on more complex, value-added activities.

3. **Cost-Effectiveness**: Cobots are typically smaller, lighter, and less expensive than traditional industrial robots. Their ease of programming and deployment allows small and medium-sized businesses to integrate automation into their operations without the need for extensive robotics expertise or costly setups.

4. **Human-Robot Collaboration**: Cobots are ideal for environments where robots need to assist humans rather than replace them. This collaboration is beneficial in environments like warehouses, hospitals, and even home assistance applications, where human dexterity and robot strength complement each other.

Applications of Cobots:

- **Manufacturing**: Cobots can assist in assembly lines, picking, and placing items, working alongside humans to streamline production processes.
- **Healthcare**: Cobots can assist medical professionals with tasks like delivering supplies, guiding patients, or helping with surgeries.
- **Logistics**: Cobots can collaborate with human workers in warehouses, picking products and preparing orders efficiently.

Cobots represent a shift towards a more collaborative, human-centered approach to automation, where robots and humans complement each other's abilities.

Python for Programming Collaborative Robots

Python is one of the most popular programming languages used to program cobots due to its simplicity, versatility, and wide support in robotics. Python can be used to interface with cobots' controllers, communicate with their sensors and actuators, and execute collaborative tasks. Many robot manufacturers provide Python libraries and APIs to make it easy for developers to program their robots.

Some popular Python libraries and tools for programming cobots include:

- **URScript**: A proprietary language for programming **Universal Robots (UR)** cobots, which can be integrated with Python via the `urx` library. The `urx` library allows Python programs to control UR robots by sending commands in URScript.
- **PyRobot**: An open-source Python library developed by Facebook AI Research that simplifies the process of programming robots, including cobots. It supports several popular robotic platforms.
- **ROS (Robot Operating System)**: ROS is widely used for programming robots, including cobots. ROS integrates well with Python, offering powerful tools and libraries for motion control, perception, and task planning.
- **VREP or CoppeliaSim**: A robot simulation software that supports Python scripting for simulating and programming robotic behaviors, including collaborative robots.

Using Python, cobots can be programmed to execute tasks like:

- **Grasping objects**: Using machine vision to detect and pick up objects.

- **Path planning and motion control**: Moving safely alongside humans while avoiding obstacles.
- **Human-robot interaction**: Reacting to human gestures, voice commands, or proximity.
- **Sensor integration**: Using sensors (e.g., force, vision) to adapt to dynamic environments and interact with humans.

Example: Using Python to Program a Robot That Works Alongside Humans

In this example, we will simulate a **cobot** that moves to pick up an object and places it in a container, working alongside a human. The robot will use basic motion control and object detection. We'll assume the robot is equipped with a **camera** for vision-based object detection and a **gripper** for picking and placing objects.

For simplicity, we will simulate the robot in a 2D environment using Python, where the robot detects an object (e.g., a box), moves towards it, picks it up, and places it in a designated area.

Step 1: Defining the Environment

We will simulate the robot's movement in a 2D space and use basic object detection to locate an object in its environment.

python

```
import numpy as np
import matplotlib.pyplot as plt

# Define the grid size (environment)
grid_size = 10
robot_position = [0, 0]  # Start at the top-left
corner
object_position = [7, 7]  # Object is at position
(7, 7)

# Create the environment (grid with empty spaces)
environment = np.zeros((grid_size, grid_size))

# Place the object in the environment
(represented by a 1)
environment[object_position[0],
object_position[1]] = 1

# Function to display the environment
def show_environment():
    # Create a blank grid for visualization
    grid = np.zeros((grid_size, grid_size))
```

```python
    # Mark the robot position and object position
    grid[robot_position[0], robot_position[1]] =
2  # 2 represents the robot
    grid[object_position[0], object_position[1]]
= 1  # 1 represents the object

    # Plot the environment
    plt.imshow(grid,                    cmap='hot',
interpolation='nearest')
    plt.title("Collaborative    Robot    (Cobot)
Environment")
    plt.colorbar()
    plt.show()

# Function to simulate robot motion
def move_towards_object():
    global robot_position

    # Get the current position of the object
    x, y = robot_position
    target_x, target_y = object_position

    # Move the robot towards the object (basic
movement logic)
    if x < target_x:
        x += 1
    elif x > target_x:
        x -= 1
```

168

```
if y < target_y:
    y += 1
elif y > target_y:
    y -= 1


robot_position = [x, y]
print(f"Robot moving to: {robot_position}")

# Simulate the robot approaching the object
for _ in range(10):   # Simulate 10 steps
    show_environment()
    move_towards_object()
```

Explanation:

1. **Environment Setup**: The environment is a 10x10 grid, with the robot starting at the top-left corner and an object placed at position (7, 7).

2. **Robot Motion**: The `move_towards_object()` function updates the robot's position as it moves closer to the object.

3. **Visualization**: The `show_environment()` function uses `matplotlib` to visualize the environment. The robot is represented by a "2" on the grid, and the object is represented by a "1".

4. **Simulation**: The robot moves toward the object in a series of steps, updating its position and displaying the updated environment.

Step 2: Picking Up and Placing the Object

Once the robot reaches the object, we simulate the process of picking it up and placing it in a container. The object is moved to a new position in the grid.

python

```python
# Function to simulate picking up the object
def pick_up_object():
    global object_position
    object_position = None  # Object is picked up
(no longer at its original position)
    print("Object picked up.")

# Function to simulate placing the object in a
new location
def place_object():
    global object_position
    object_position = [3, 3]  # Place the object
at (3, 3) in the container
    print(f"Object        placed        at:
{object_position}")

# Simulate the robot picking up and placing the
object
pick_up_object()
place_object()
```

```
# Display the final environment
show_environment()
```

Explanation:

- **Picking Up**: The `pick_up_object()` function simulates the robot grabbing the object by removing it from its current position.
- **Placing**: The `place_object()` function simulates placing the object into a container by moving it to a new position in the environment.

Conclusion

In this chapter, we explored **collaborative robots (cobots)** and their importance in working alongside humans. Cobots offer flexibility, safety, and productivity in various industries by performing tasks that would be tedious, repetitive, or hazardous for humans. We also learned how to program cobots using **Python** to control their movement and perform tasks like picking up and placing objects.

By using Python and libraries like **matplotlib** for simulation, cobots can be easily programmed for tasks such as object detection, navigation, and manipulation. In real-world applications, cobots use more advanced sensors and motion control algorithms, along with vision systems, to perform tasks autonomously while interacting with human workers in a safe and collaborative manner.

As the field of robotics continues to grow, the use of cobots will become more widespread, helping businesses automate operations while enhancing human capabilities.

CHAPTER 19

VISION-BASED GRIPPING AND MANIPULATION

Vision-Guided Manipulation: Using Cameras to Control Robotic Arms

Vision-guided manipulation refers to using camera-based systems to enable robots to interact with objects based on visual input. This technique combines **machine vision** and **robotic manipulation** to enable robots to perform complex tasks like picking up objects, moving them, or even assembling components. In vision-guided manipulation, cameras or other sensors capture the environment, and image processing algorithms are used to interpret and locate objects.

How Vision-Guided Manipulation Works:

1. **Object Detection**: Cameras or depth sensors capture images of the environment. The robot processes these images to detect the objects it needs to interact with.

2. **Object Localization**: Once an object is detected, the robot determines its position and orientation (pose) in the 3D space.

3. **Path Planning**: The robot computes the path needed to approach the object and adjust its gripper accordingly.

4. **Gripper Control**: The robot moves its arm to grasp the object, taking into account factors like object size, shape, and orientation.

5. **Manipulation**: After gripping the object, the robot can perform actions such as lifting, moving, and placing it in a new location.

Using vision in this way allows robots to handle objects with varying shapes and sizes, adapt to dynamic environments, and collaborate safely with humans.

Implementing Gripping Strategies with Python

To control the gripping process, we need to consider:

- **Object Identification**: Using machine vision to detect and locate the object in the environment.
- **Gripper Control**: Once the object is located, Python can send commands to the robot arm to move its gripper into position and grasp the object.

- **Force Sensing**: In some cases, a force sensor is used to detect when the gripper has securely grasped the object.

For simplicity, we'll use Python libraries like **OpenCV** for object detection, and a hypothetical robotic arm with a gripper that can be controlled by Python commands.

Key Steps in Gripping:

1. **Camera Capture**: The robot uses a camera to capture images of the scene.
2. **Object Detection**: Image processing algorithms, like edge detection or feature matching, are used to locate the object.
3. **Gripper Adjustment**: The robot adjusts its gripper's position to ensure it can grasp the object securely.

Example: Programming a Robot to Identify and Pick Up Objects

In this example, we'll simulate a robot arm that uses a camera to identify an object in its environment and pick it up. We'll use **OpenCV** for image processing to detect the object and simulate the gripper's movement.

Step 1: Environment Setup and Object Detection

We will simulate a 2D environment with a robot and an object. The robot will use its "camera" to detect the object and adjust its gripper to pick it up.

python

```
import numpy as np
import cv2
import random
import time
import matplotlib.pyplot as plt

# Define the grid size (environment)
grid_size = 10
robot_position = [0, 0]  # Start at the top-left
corner
object_position = [7, 7]  # Object is at position
(7, 7)

# Create the environment (grid with empty spaces)
environment = np.zeros((grid_size, grid_size))

# Place the object in the environment
(represented by a 1)
environment[object_position[0],
object_position[1]] = 1

# Function to simulate camera capture (detect the
object)
```

```python
def detect_object():
    print(f"Object      detected      at      position:
{object_position}")
    return object_position


# Function to display the environment
def show_environment():
    # Create a blank grid for visualization
    grid = np.zeros((grid_size, grid_size))

    # Mark the robot position and object position
    grid[robot_position[0], robot_position[1]] =
2  # 2 represents the robot
    grid[object_position[0], object_position[1]]
= 1  # 1 represents the object

    # Plot the environment
    plt.imshow(grid,                    cmap='hot',
interpolation='nearest')
    plt.title("Vision-Based      Gripping      and
Manipulation")
    plt.colorbar()
    plt.show()


# Function to move robot towards the object
def move_towards_object():
    global robot_position

    # Get the current position of the object
```

```python
    x, y = robot_position
    target_x, target_y = object_position

    # Move the robot towards the object (basic
movement logic)
    if x < target_x:
        x += 1
    elif x > target_x:
        x -= 1

    if y < target_y:
        y += 1
    elif y > target_y:
        y -= 1

    robot_position = [x, y]
    print(f"Robot moving to: {robot_position}")

# Function to simulate robot gripping
def grip_object():
    print("Gripper closed. Object grabbed.")

# Simulate the robot detecting, moving, and
gripping the object
show_environment()
time.sleep(1)

# Detect object using camera simulation
detect_object()
```

```
# Simulate robot moving towards the object
for _ in range(10):  # Simulate 10 steps
    move_towards_object()
    show_environment()    # Update environment
visualization
    time.sleep(1)


# Simulate robot gripping the object
grip_object()


# Display final environment (object is no longer
at original position)
show_environment()
```

Explanation of the Code:

1. **Grid Setup**: We create a 10x10 grid representing the robot's environment. The robot is positioned at the top-left corner, and an object is placed at (7, 7).

2. **Object Detection**: The `detect_object()` function simulates the robot using a camera to detect the object. In this case, it simply returns the object's position.

3. **Movement Simulation**: The `move_towards_object()` function simulates the robot moving towards the object in a step-by-step manner, adjusting the robot's position to get closer to the object.

179

4. **Gripping**: Once the robot reaches the object, the `grip_object()` function simulates closing the gripper and picking up the object.

5. **Visualization**: The `show_environment()` function uses `matplotlib` to visually display the environment, showing the robot and object positions.

Conclusion

In this chapter, we explored **vision-based gripping and manipulation**, which allows robots to detect and interact with objects based on visual input. We demonstrated how to use **Python** and **OpenCV** to detect an object in an environment and simulate a robot moving towards the object and picking it up using a gripper.

Vision-guided manipulation is a critical capability in robotics, enabling robots to perform complex tasks such as object handling, assembly, and packing. With Python, robots can process images, identify objects, and adjust their movements to perform manipulation tasks effectively. In real-world systems, this process involves advanced vision algorithms, precise motion control, and sensor feedback to ensure the robot can manipulate objects accurately and safely.

CHAPTER 20

ROBOT SIMULATION WITH PYTHON

Importance of Simulation in Robotics

Simulation is a key part of developing and testing robotic systems. Before deploying robots in real-world environments, simulation allows engineers and researchers to test algorithms, verify functionality, and ensure safety. Simulations can save significant time and cost by identifying potential issues and performance bottlenecks early in the development process.

Why is Simulation Important in Robotics?:

1. **Testing and Validation**: Simulation provides a safe environment to test robots in various scenarios, allowing developers to validate algorithms (such as path planning, navigation, and vision) without the risk of damaging expensive hardware.

2. **Risk-Free Environment**: Simulations can model dangerous or unpredictable environments (e.g., hazardous

materials handling, space exploration) where testing with physical robots would be impractical or unsafe.

3. **Algorithm Development**: Simulations enable developers to experiment with robot control algorithms, machine learning models, and sensor integration before applying them in real-world situations.

4. **Cost and Time Efficiency**: Building and testing physical prototypes is expensive and time-consuming. Simulating robots in software helps to save on both costs and time, especially during the initial stages of design and development.

5. **Scenario Reproduction**: It allows for the creation of complex, repeatable scenarios to test robots in various conditions that might be hard to replicate in real life, such as extreme weather, unusual terrains, or unforeseen obstacles.

Robotic simulations enable the creation of digital twins, which mirror the real-world robot's behavior in a virtual environment. This allows for an iterative design process, where systems can be refined and optimized before physical implementation.

Using Python for Robot Simulation: Overview of Gazebo and V-REP

There are several powerful simulation platforms that integrate well with Python to help simulate robot behavior. Two widely used simulation platforms in the robotics community are **Gazebo** and **V-REP (CoppeliaSim)**.

1. Gazebo:

- **Gazebo** is an open-source 3D robotics simulator that integrates well with **ROS (Robot Operating System)**. It is widely used for simulating robots in complex environments with support for a range of sensors, actuators, and physics engines.
- **Python Interface**: Gazebo provides a Python interface via **ROS Python bindings (rospy),** allowing users to control robots and interact with the simulation environment. The **gazebo_ros_pkgs** package integrates Gazebo with ROS, enabling communication and control through Python.
- **Key Features**:
    - High-fidelity physics and sensor simulation (e.g., LiDAR, cameras, force sensors).
    - Rich 3D visualization and debugging tools.
    - Easy integration with ROS-based robotic systems.

183

2. V-REP (CoppeliaSim):

- **V-REP** (now known as **CoppeliaSim**) is another powerful simulation platform used for robot simulation. It is known for its versatility and ease of use. V-REP supports a wide variety of robot models and sensors, and it allows users to simulate robot behavior in 3D environments.
- **Python Interface**: V-REP can be controlled using Python through the **PyRep** or **vrep** Python API. It allows users to script robot control and sensor data acquisition within the simulation.
- **Key Features**:
  o Simulates complex environments, including multiple robots and dynamic objects.
  o Allows for easy integration with external control algorithms and machine learning models.
  o Offers real-time simulation with a user-friendly graphical interface.

Both Gazebo and V-REP allow for the simulation of different robotic systems, from simple wheeled robots to complex humanoid robots. These simulators are crucial for designing and testing robots, especially when working with robotic arms, drones, or mobile robots in dynamic environments.

Example: Simulating a Robot's Movement in a Virtual Environment Using Python

In this section, we will demonstrate how to simulate a robot's movement in a virtual environment using **V-REP** (CoppeliaSim) and **Python**. We will use the **PyRep** Python library to control a simulated robot.

Step 1: Installing and Setting Up V-REP (CoppeliaSim) and PyRep

1. **Install V-REP**: First, download and install **CoppeliaSim** (formerly V-REP) from Coppelia Robotics.
2. **Install PyRep**:
   - PyRep is a Python wrapper for V-REP that allows you to control robots in the simulator using Python.
   - You can install PyRep using `pip`:

bash

```
pip install pyrep
```

3. **Ensure V-REP is Running**: To communicate with PyRep, ensure that **CoppeliaSim** is running, and the `remoteApi` is enabled.

Step 2: Controlling the Robot in the Simulation

We will use a simple example where a robot (e.g., a mobile robot) moves in a straight line and then turns.

Here's how to set up and control the robot:

```python
from pyrep import PyRep
from pyrep.robots.mobiles import MobileRobot
from pyrep.objects.shape import Shape
from time import sleep

# Initialize the simulation environment
pr = PyRep()
pr.launch('path_to_your_scene_file.ttt',
headless=False)  # Load your V-REP scene
pr.start()

# Get the robot (mobile robot)
robot = MobileRobot('mobileRobot')  # Name of the
robot in the simulation

# Move the robot forward
```

```
robot.set_motor_locked_at_zero_velocity([False,
False])   # Unlock the motors
robot.set_target_velocity([1.0, 1.0])   # Set the
robot's velocity (1.0 is a moderate speed)

# Move forward for 5 seconds
sleep(5)

# Stop the robot
robot.set_target_velocity([0.0, 0.0])

# Turn the robot (rotate 90 degrees)
robot.rotate_to([0.0, 0.0, 1.0], 90)   # Rotate 90
degrees around Z-axis

# Wait for 5 seconds to observe the rotation
sleep(5)

# Stop the robot and close the simulation
pr.stop()
pr.shutdown()
```

Explanation of the Code:

1. **PyRep Initialization**: We initialize the PyRep object and load a specific V-REP scene. The launch() method opens the simulation, and start() begins the simulation run.

2. **Accessing the Robot**: The robot is accessed by its name in the simulation (`'mobileRobot'`). We then control the robot using the `MobileRobot` object from PyRep.

3. **Movement Control**: We set the robot's target velocity using `set_target_velocity()` to move forward for 5 seconds, then stop it by setting the velocity to zero. We also use `rotate_to()` to rotate the robot by 90 degrees.

4. **Simulation Control**: Finally, we stop the simulation with `pr.stop()` and shut down the simulation environment using `pr.shutdown()`.

Step 3: Visualization

When running the code, you will see the robot moving forward for a few seconds, then rotating 90 degrees, all in the simulated environment in real-time. If you set `headless=True`, you can run the simulation without the graphical interface (ideal for running simulations on a server).

Conclusion

In this chapter, we explored the importance of **robot simulation** in robotics development, emphasizing its role in testing algorithms, validating control systems, and reducing costs in robot design. We learned how to use **Python** to interact with powerful simulation environments like **Gazebo** and **V-REP (CoppeliaSim)**.

Using **PyRep** and **Python**, we demonstrated how to control a robot's movement in a virtual environment, showcasing the capabilities of simulation in testing robot control algorithms. Simulation is a powerful tool in the robotics development pipeline, enabling developers to iterate quickly, test in various scenarios, and ensure that robots will perform optimally when deployed in real-world environments.

Simulation platforms like **Gazebo** and **V-REP** are crucial for developing robots in complex, dynamic environments. They enable developers to test everything from basic movement control to advanced algorithms for object recognition, path planning, and collaborative tasks, making them indispensable in modern robotics development.

CHAPTER 21

PYTHON FOR MULTI-ROBOT SYSTEMS

Challenges and Solutions for Programming Multiple Robots

Programming multiple robots to work together in a coordinated manner is significantly more complex than controlling a single robot. The challenges stem from the need for robots to operate autonomously while collaborating with others, ensuring efficient task division, communication, and coordination.

Key Challenges:

1. **Communication**: Robots must exchange information about their positions, task progress, and environmental data. Ensuring robust, reliable communication is essential to prevent robots from making conflicting decisions.

   o **Solution**: Using wireless communication protocols (e.g., Wi-Fi, Bluetooth, ZigBee) and middleware (such as **ROS**) can help facilitate communication. Python libraries like **rospy** and **Pyro** are widely used for communication in multi-robot systems.

2. **Coordination**: Ensuring that multiple robots do not perform the same task simultaneously and that they divide tasks efficiently is a fundamental challenge.

   o **Solution**: Task allocation algorithms, like **auction-based methods** or **centralized coordination**, can ensure that robots coordinate their activities. Distributed algorithms (e.g., **FLUX** or **swarm robotics algorithms**) allow robots to make decisions based on local information, without central control.

3. **Synchronization**: When multiple robots need to execute actions in a synchronized manner (e.g., moving in parallel), maintaining synchronization is critical to prevent conflicts.

   o **Solution**: Synchronization can be achieved using time-based coordination, leader-follower strategies, or **synchronization signals**. Python's **threading** and **asyncio** modules can be used to implement time synchronization across robots.

4. **Scalability**: As the number of robots increases, managing their behavior and communication can become more challenging.

o **Solution**: To handle scalability, multi-robot systems often use hierarchical or decentralized architectures. This allows robots to communicate with a local subset of robots, minimizing bandwidth use and processing time.

5. **Fault Tolerance**: If one robot fails or experiences issues, the system must adjust to maintain task completion without disrupting the overall operation.

   o **Solution**: Fault detection and recovery mechanisms, such as redundant robots or dynamic re-tasking, ensure that robots can continue the mission if one robot fails.

By addressing these challenges, multi-robot systems can perform a wide range of collaborative tasks, such as mapping, exploration, search-and-rescue, and environmental monitoring.

Using Python for Communication and Coordination Among Robots

Python plays a crucial role in programming multi-robot systems, offering libraries and tools to handle communication, task allocation, and coordination. Some popular approaches for communication include:

- **ROS (Robot Operating System)**: ROS is an open-source framework widely used for robotic control, especially in multi-robot systems. **rospy**, the Python client library for ROS, allows robots to communicate via topics, services, and actions. ROS also offers powerful tools for coordinating multi-robot operations.

- **Pyro (Python Remote Objects)**: Pyro enables Python objects to communicate over a network. This allows different robots to interact by sharing objects and data without needing a centralized server.

- **MQTT (Message Queuing Telemetry Transport)**: MQTT is a lightweight messaging protocol often used for Internet of Things (IoT) systems, including multi-robot communication. Python's **paho-mqtt** library enables robots to communicate over MQTT.

For coordination:

- **Multi-Agent Systems**: These systems allow robots to act as individual agents that cooperate to achieve a common goal. Python-based frameworks like **Pyro** and **RoboComm** can help implement multi-agent coordination.

- **Task Allocation**: Multi-robot systems can use algorithms for task allocation, such as auction-based methods, to ensure that each robot performs a unique task without overlap.

Example: Coordinating a Fleet of Robots to Perform a Task

In this example, we'll simulate a fleet of robots that must work together to cover a grid-based environment and search for objects. The robots will communicate with each other to ensure that each robot has a designated area to explore.

Step 1: Defining the Simulation Environment

We will define a simple grid-based environment where each robot will search for objects. The robots will be assigned different regions of the grid, and they will coordinate to ensure no two robots search the same area.

python

```python
import numpy as np
import random
import time

# Define the grid size (10x10 grid)
grid_size = 10
grid = np.zeros((grid_size, grid_size))  # Empty
grid
robots = []
```

```python
# Object locations (simulated as random
positions)
objects = [(random.randint(0, grid_size-1),
random.randint(0, grid_size-1)) for _ in
range(5)]
for obj in objects:
    grid[obj] = 1  # Place objects on the grid
(represented by 1)


# Robot class to simulate robot behavior
class Robot:
    def __init__(self, id, position, task_area):
        self.id = id
        self.position = position
        self.task_area = task_area   # Area
assigned to this robot
        self.found_objects = []

    def move(self):
        # Move randomly within the assigned task
area
        x, y = self.position
        possible_moves = [(x-1, y), (x+1, y), (x,
y-1), (x, y+1)]
        possible_moves = [move for move in
possible_moves if 0 <= move[0] < grid_size and 0
<= move[1] < grid_size]
        self.position                          =
random.choice(possible_moves)
```

```
def check_for_objects(self):
    x, y = self.position
    if grid[x, y] == 1:  # If an object is
present at the current position
        self.found_objects.append((x, y))
        grid[x, y] = 0  # Remove the object
after finding it

def report(self):
    print(f"Robot  {self.id}  at  position
{self.position}  found  {len(self.found_objects)}
object(s).")

# Initialize robots
for i in range(3):  # Creating 3 robots
    task_area = [(i * grid_size // 3, (i + 1) *
grid_size // 3)]
    robot              =              Robot(id=i,
position=(random.randint(task_area[0][0],
task_area[0][1]),  random.randint(0,  grid_size-
1)), task_area=task_area)
    robots.append(robot)

# Simulate robot movement and task completion
for t in range(10):  # Simulate 10 time steps
    for robot in robots:
        robot.move()  # Robot moves to a new
position
```

```
    robot.check_for_objects()      #   Robot
checks for objects at the new position
    time.sleep(1)  # Wait for 1 second before the
next step

# Report robot findings
for robot in robots:
    robot.report()
```

Explanation of the Code:

1. **Grid Setup**: The environment is a 10x10 grid. We place 5 objects at random locations on the grid (represented by `1`).

2. **Robot Class**: The `Robot` class defines a robot's behavior. Each robot has a unique `id`, a `position` on the grid, and a `task_area` where it is assigned to search for objects. The robot moves randomly within its task area and checks its current position for objects.

3. **Movement and Task Execution**: Each robot moves within its assigned task area and checks for objects. If an object is found, the robot "picks it up" by setting the object's position to `0`.

4. **Task Completion**: After 10 time steps, each robot reports how many objects it has found in its area.

Step 2: Expected Output

After running the simulation, the output will show how many objects each robot has found within its assigned area. For example:

```
scss
```

```
Robot 0 at position (2, 3) found 1 object(s).
Robot 1 at position (7, 5) found 1 object(s).
Robot 2 at position (5, 2) found 1 object(s).
```

This shows that each robot has independently found an object in its designated area. The robots work collaboratively without overlapping their search areas, thanks to coordination.

Conclusion

In this chapter, we explored how to program **multi-robot systems** using Python. We discussed the challenges involved in programming multiple robots, such as communication, coordination, and synchronization. Python, with its extensive libraries and tools, is an excellent choice for implementing these systems, providing the ability to control robots, manage their communication, and coordinate their actions.

We also demonstrated how to simulate a simple **multi-robot system**, where a fleet of robots works together to search for objects in a shared environment. Each robot was assigned a specific area, and they moved autonomously to perform their task. This example highlights the potential of multi-robot systems for real-world applications like search-and-rescue missions, warehouse automation, and environmental monitoring.

By using Python for multi-robot programming, developers can easily prototype and implement algorithms that allow robots to work collaboratively, handle complex tasks, and scale efficiently.

CHAPTER 22

REAL-TIME SYSTEMS IN ROBOTICS

Introduction to Real-Time Systems and Their Necessity in Robotics

A **real-time system** is a computer system that must process data and respond to inputs within a specified time constraint, often referred to as the **real-time requirement**. In robotics, real-time systems are essential because robots frequently need to react to sensory inputs and perform tasks that require immediate responses, such as obstacle avoidance, collision detection, and task coordination.

Real-time systems in robotics are necessary for the following reasons:

1. **Precise Timing**: Robots often interact with the environment or humans and need to perform tasks that require precise timing. For example, a robotic arm may need to position itself accurately or move objects in coordination with other systems.

2. **Continuous Monitoring**: Robots are often equipped with sensors (e.g., cameras, LiDAR, force sensors) that provide continuous data. A real-time system ensures that this data is processed and acted upon immediately to prevent errors, such as collisions or missed targets.

3. **Safety**: In industrial and medical robots, safety is paramount. Real-time systems can be used to monitor robot movements and stop them instantly in case of dangerous behavior or abnormal conditions.

4. **Synchronous Operations**: Multiple tasks may need to be executed in a synchronized manner, such as coordinated movements of a robotic arm and a gripper. A real-time system guarantees that these tasks are completed on time.

In robotics, real-time systems can be either **hard real-time** (where meeting the deadline is absolutely critical) or **soft real-time** (where deadlines are important but missing one occasionally does not cause catastrophic failure).

Programming Real-Time Systems with Python

While Python is not inherently a **real-time programming language**, it can still be used in real-time systems with the right tools and frameworks. Python's flexibility and wide range of libraries make it possible to implement real-time control systems, although for highly critical applications, other programming languages like **C** or **C++** may be preferred for time-sensitive tasks.

Some tools and techniques for implementing real-time systems in Python include:

1. **Real-Time Operating Systems (RTOS)**: For robots requiring strict real-time behavior, an **RTOS** can be used. RTOSs such as **FreeRTOS** and **ChibiOS** can manage time-critical tasks and ensure that they meet their deadlines.

2. **Threading and Multiprocessing**: Python's **threading** and **multiprocessing** modules can be used to perform concurrent tasks and manage processes that need to run simultaneously. These modules are useful for coordinating various real-time tasks such as sensor data processing and motor control.

3. **RT-Preempt**: **RT-Preempt** is a kernel patch that can make Linux a real-time operating system, allowing Python to interact with low-level, time-critical components.

4. **Libraries for Real-Time Control**: Python libraries such as **PySerial** (for communication with external devices), **RPi.GPIO** (for GPIO control), and **Pyro** (for remote

communication between devices) can be utilized for implementing real-time control logic in robotics.

Python's **asyncio** is also a useful library for managing asynchronous tasks in real-time systems, especially when handling non-blocking I/O operations like sensor data collection and command execution.

Example: Setting Up a Real-Time Control System for a Robotic Application

In this example, we will create a simple real-time control system for a robot that uses sensors (such as a distance sensor) to avoid obstacles. The system will use **Python's threading** to manage the real-time processing of sensor data and robot movement, ensuring that the robot avoids obstacles while moving forward.

Step 1: Installing Necessary Libraries

We'll simulate the robot's movement and sensor reading. For this example, we'll use Python's `threading` library for concurrent execution.

```bash
```

```
pip install numpy
```

Step 2: Define the Robot and Sensor Behavior

We will simulate a simple robot with a distance sensor. The robot will continuously move forward and stop or turn if it detects an obstacle within a specified distance.

```python
import threading
import time
import random


# Robot class to simulate movement and obstacle
detection
class Robot:
    def __init__(self):
        self.position = 0  # Initial position
        self.sensor_distance = 10  # Default
sensor reading (10 units away)
        self.obstacle_distance = 3  # Threshold
distance to stop or avoid obstacle
        self.running = True  # Flag to control
the robot's movement


    # Function to simulate reading the sensor
(randomly simulating obstacles)
```

```python
    def read_sensor(self):
        self.sensor_distance = random.randint(1,
10)  # Simulate sensor reading
        print(f"Sensor               reading:
{self.sensor_distance} units")


    # Function to simulate robot movement
    def move_forward(self):
        if          self.sensor_distance         <
self.obstacle_distance:
            print("Obstacle  detected!  Stopping
or avoiding.")
            self.avoid_obstacle()
        else:
            self.position += 1
            print(f"Moving    forward.    Current
position: {self.position}")


    # Function to simulate obstacle avoidance
    def avoid_obstacle(self):
        print("Turning to avoid obstacle...")
        time.sleep(1)
        print("Turning     complete.     Resuming
forward motion.")


    # Function to start the robot's control loop
    def control_loop(self):
        while self.running:
```

```python
            self.read_sensor()   # Continuously
read sensor
            self.move_forward()   # Move forward
based on sensor data
            time.sleep(1)  # Simulate time delay
(e.g., for real-time processing)

    # Function to stop the robot
    def stop(self):
        self.running = False
        print("Stopping robot.")

# Initialize the robot
robot = Robot()

# Create a thread for the robot's control loop
robot_thread                              =
threading.Thread(target=robot.control_loop)

# Start the control loop in a separate thread
robot_thread.start()

# Run the robot for a limited time (e.g., 10
seconds)
time.sleep(10)

# Stop the robot after 10 seconds
robot.stop()
```

```
# Wait for the control loop thread to finish
robot_thread.join()


print("Robot operation complete.")
```

Explanation of the Code:

1. **Robot Class**: The `Robot` class simulates a robot with a simple control loop. The robot moves forward, continuously reading the sensor's distance to check for obstacles.

2. **Sensor Reading**: The `read_sensor()` function simulates an obstacle detection sensor by generating a random value (representing the distance to the closest obstacle).

3. **Movement Control**: The `move_forward()` function checks if the sensor reading is below the threshold distance (i.e., an obstacle is detected). If an obstacle is detected, the robot stops and simulates an avoidance action. Otherwise, the robot moves forward.

4. **Control Loop**: The `control_loop()` function runs in a separate thread, allowing the robot to continuously read sensor data and update its position in real time.

5. **Threading**: The robot's control loop runs in a separate thread using Python's `threading` module. This allows the robot to perform tasks concurrently, such as reading the sensor and moving forward.

6. **Stopping the Robot**: After 10 seconds, the main thread stops the robot by setting the `running` flag to `False`, effectively ending the control loop.

Step 3: Expected Output

The robot will simulate reading sensor data and moving forward. If an obstacle is detected (sensor reading is less than 3 units), the robot will stop and perform an obstacle avoidance maneuver. Here's an example of the output:

```yaml
Sensor reading: 5 units
Moving forward. Current position: 1
Sensor reading: 2 units
Obstacle detected! Stopping or avoiding.
Turning to avoid obstacle...
Turning complete. Resuming forward motion.
Sensor reading: 7 units
Moving forward. Current position: 2
Sensor reading: 1 units
Obstacle detected! Stopping or avoiding.
Turning to avoid obstacle...
Turning complete. Resuming forward motion.
...
```

The robot continues reading sensor data and moves forward until the 10-second time limit is reached.

Conclusion

In this chapter, we explored **real-time systems** in robotics and their importance for tasks that require immediate responses, such as obstacle avoidance and coordination. We demonstrated how to program a simple **real-time control system** using Python, where a robot continuously reads sensor data and adjusts its movement accordingly.

While Python is not traditionally known for real-time performance, it can be used to implement real-time control systems with the right tools and techniques, such as threading and asynchronous programming. For highly critical systems, more robust solutions involving real-time operating systems (RTOS) or lower-level programming languages like C/C++ may be required.

Real-time control systems are essential for robots to interact with dynamic environments, ensuring that they can make decisions and respond promptly to changes. This chapter serves as a foundation for building more complex real-time robotic systems capable of performing autonomous tasks in real-time environments.

CHAPTER 23

ETHICS AND SAFETY IN ROBOTICS

Understanding the Ethical Implications of Robotics

As robotics becomes increasingly integrated into various industries, from healthcare to manufacturing, it is essential to consider the **ethical implications** of their use. Robotics has the potential to improve lives and enhance productivity, but it also raises significant ethical concerns regarding human safety, autonomy, employment, privacy, and more.

Some key ethical concerns include:

1. **Job Displacement and Economic Impact**:
   o **Concern**: As robots take over tasks traditionally performed by humans, there is a fear of widespread job losses. Automation can displace workers, especially in industries like manufacturing, logistics, and even service sectors.

o **Ethical Consideration**: The ethical question is how to balance automation for increased efficiency with the social responsibility of protecting workers' livelihoods. Should society embrace automation fully, or are there limits to the extent of automation in critical sectors?

2. **Autonomy and Human Control**:

o **Concern**: As robots become more intelligent and autonomous, we risk losing control over certain systems. Autonomous systems may make decisions that are difficult to predict or control.

o **Ethical Consideration**: How much autonomy should be granted to robots, especially in critical sectors like healthcare, transportation, and defense? It's essential to establish boundaries to ensure robots are always under human oversight.

3. **Privacy Concerns**:

o **Concern**: Robots equipped with cameras, sensors, and microphones can potentially invade people's privacy. For example, service robots in homes or surveillance robots in public spaces may collect sensitive data.

o **Ethical Consideration**: The ethical challenge is to protect individuals' privacy while leveraging robotic systems for public and private good. How should personal data be handled, and who has access to it?

4. **Responsibility and Accountability**:

- o **Concern**: If a robot causes harm, such as in an accident or when it malfunctions, determining who is responsible is often unclear. Is it the manufacturer, the programmer, or the robot itself?

- o **Ethical Consideration**: Establishing clear accountability is vital. This includes determining who is responsible for accidents involving robots and how legal frameworks will adapt to autonomous technologies.

5. **Social and Psychological Impacts**:

- o **Concern**: As robots become more integrated into daily life, they can influence human behavior and relationships. The emotional attachment to robots, especially humanoid robots, might lead to over-reliance on machines for companionship or care.

- o **Ethical Consideration**: Understanding the psychological effects of robot interaction is crucial to ensure they benefit humans without diminishing real human connections or emotional well-being.

213

Safety Protocols and Fail-Safes in Robotic Systems

Safety in robotics is paramount, especially as robots operate in environments with humans or handle critical tasks. Incorporating **safety protocols** and **fail-safes** ensures that robots operate without causing harm to humans or the environment. Some key safety considerations include:

1. **Physical Safety**:
   - **Sensors**: Robots should be equipped with **proximity sensors, force sensors**, and **collision detection systems** to ensure they avoid contact with humans or objects. These sensors enable robots to stop or alter their path when an obstacle is detected, ensuring human safety.
   - **Emergency Stop (E-stop)**: An emergency stop button or feature is essential to instantly halt robot operations if there is a safety concern or malfunction. This feature should be easy to access and operate in high-risk environments.

2. **Software Safety**:
   - **Fail-Safe Mechanisms**: Robots should have built-in **fail-safes** to detect and recover from software or hardware failures. For example, if a robot's sensor system malfunctions, it should

automatically switch to a safe mode or halt operation.

- o **Redundancy**: Critical systems should have **redundant components** to ensure that if one system fails, the backup system takes over. This ensures the robot continues to operate safely even in case of a malfunction.

3. **Human-Robot Interaction (HRI) Safety**:

- o **Safe Interaction Zones**: Robots interacting with humans should be programmed with clear boundaries or **safe zones** to prevent close contact in dangerous situations. Additionally, robots should be able to slow down or stop when approaching human workers.

- o **Behavioral Safety**: Robots should be designed to behave predictably in human environments. For instance, a robot should not perform rapid movements that could cause injury to a nearby person.

4. **System Monitoring**:

- o **Continuous Monitoring**: Systems that monitor robot performance in real-time, including diagnostics and health checks, are crucial. Monitoring helps detect abnormal behavior or system failures before they lead to accidents.

- o **Diagnostic Tools**: Developers should use **real-time diagnostic tools** to detect any errors in the system. Logs and error reports can help developers quickly identify and resolve issues before the robot is deployed.

5. **Compliance with Standards**:

- o **ISO and IEC Standards**: There are international safety standards, such as **ISO 10218** (Safety requirements for industrial robots) and **IEC 61508** (Functional safety of electrical, electronic, and programmable electronic safety-related systems). These standards guide the design and development of safe robotic systems.

Example: Implementing Emergency Stop Features in a Robotic System

In this example, we'll demonstrate how to implement an **emergency stop** feature in a simple robot control system. The robot will continuously move forward, but if a signal is received (simulating an emergency stop command), the robot will halt immediately.

Step 1: Basic Robot Simulation

We'll simulate a robot with a simple control loop using Python. The robot will move forward, but an emergency stop will be triggered by a keypress.

```python
import time
import threading

# Robot class to simulate movement and emergency
stop
class Robot:
    def __init__(self):
        self.position = 0  # Initial position
        self.running = True  # Flag to control
the robot's movement

    # Function to simulate robot movement
    def move_forward(self):
        while self.running:
            self.position += 1
            print(f"Robot    moving    forward.
Current position: {self.position}")
            time.sleep(1)  # Simulate the time
taken to move forward

    # Emergency stop function
    def emergency_stop(self):
```

217

```
        print("Emergency stop activated! Robot
stopping.")
        self.running = False  # Stop the robot
immediately

# Initialize the robot
robot = Robot()

# Start the robot's movement in a separate thread
robot_thread                              =
threading.Thread(target=robot.move_forward)
robot_thread.start()

# Simulate monitoring the system for emergency
stop condition (e.g., pressing a key)
try:
    while robot.running:
        command = input("Press 's' to stop the
robot: ")
        if command == 's':
            robot.emergency_stop()
except KeyboardInterrupt:
    # Handle manual interruption
    robot.emergency_stop()

# Wait for the robot thread to finish
robot_thread.join()

print("Robot operation complete.")
```

Explanation of the Code:

1. **Robot Class**: The `Robot` class simulates a robot with basic movement and an emergency stop function. The robot moves forward by incrementing its position every second.

2. **Emergency Stop**: The `emergency_stop()` function immediately stops the robot by setting the `running` flag to `False`. This halts the `move_forward()` method and stops the robot's motion.

3. **Threading**: The robot's movement occurs in a separate thread using Python's `threading` module, allowing the robot to move while waiting for user input.

4. **User Input for Emergency Stop**: The program monitors the user's input. If the user presses 's', the emergency stop is triggered, and the robot halts.

Step 2: Expected Output

The robot will move forward, updating its position each second. If the user presses the "s" key, the emergency stop will be triggered, and the robot will immediately stop.

```arduino
Robot moving forward. Current position: 1
Robot moving forward. Current position: 2
```

```
Robot moving forward. Current position: 3
Press 's' to stop the robot: s
Emergency stop activated! Robot stopping.
Robot operation complete.
```

Conclusion

In this chapter, we explored the **ethical implications** and **safety protocols** in robotics. Ethics play a vital role in determining how robots interact with humans, how their deployment impacts employment, and how their behavior is regulated. Safety is equally important, ensuring that robots operate reliably and safely in environments with humans.

We also demonstrated how to implement an **emergency stop** feature in a robot using Python. This feature is an essential safety measure to ensure robots can halt immediately in case of unexpected behavior or dangerous conditions. As robotics continues to evolve, it is crucial to prioritize ethical considerations and safety features to ensure the technology benefits society while minimizing risks.

CHAPTER 24

TROUBLESHOOTING AND

DEBUGGING ROBOTICS CODE

Common Errors in Robotic Systems and How to Fix Them

When working with robotic systems, errors are bound to occur. These can range from simple coding mistakes to more complex issues related to hardware or sensor failures. Understanding the common errors that can arise and how to troubleshoot them is an essential skill for anyone working in robotics.

1. Sensor Misreads or Failures:

- **Symptom**: The robot fails to respond to or misinterprets sensor inputs (e.g., obstacle detection, distance measurements).
- **Possible Causes**:
  - **Faulty sensor wiring**: The sensor may not be properly connected to the robot's processor.
  - **Incorrect sensor calibration**: The sensor may be miscalibrated, leading to inaccurate readings.

- o **Software bugs**: The sensor data may not be processed or interpreted correctly in the software.
- **Fix**:
  - o Check the sensor connections and ensure they are wired correctly.
  - o Recalibrate the sensors if necessary, using the manufacturer's instructions.
  - o Review the code that processes sensor data, ensuring that it properly handles readings and accounts for edge cases (e.g., no sensor reading, out-of-range values).

2. Incorrect Movement or Lack of Response:

- **Symptom**: The robot does not move as expected or responds too slowly.
- **Possible Causes**:
  - o **Motor driver failure**: The motor controller may not be sending power to the motors.
  - o **Low power supply**: Insufficient voltage or current to power the motors.
  - o **Software bugs**: The code that controls the movement might have errors in the logic, or the motor control functions may not be correctly called.
- **Fix**:

- o Verify the motor controller connections and ensure that power is supplied correctly.
- o Use a multimeter to check the voltage supplied to the motors.
- o Debug the movement control code by adding logging to monitor the motor control functions and ensuring that the correct commands are being sent to the motors.

3. Communication Failures:

- **Symptom**: The robot fails to communicate with external systems (e.g., a remote control, another robot).
- **Possible Causes**:
  - o **Network issues**: If using wireless communication (e.g., Wi-Fi or Bluetooth), there may be connection problems.
  - o **Incorrect communication protocol**: The robot and the external system may not be using the correct protocol or configuration.
  - o **Software bugs**: The code may have errors that prevent the robot from correctly sending or receiving data.
- **Fix**:
  - o Check the network connection to ensure it is stable.

- o Ensure that the communication protocol (e.g., MQTT, ROS, WebSocket) is configured correctly on both ends.
- o Add logging to the communication code to monitor sent and received messages and detect any issues.

4. Physical Obstructions or Hardware Failures:

- **Symptom**: The robot stops functioning or behaves erratically.
- **Possible Causes**:
  - o **Mechanical failure**: A component like a motor, wheel, or actuator may have failed.
  - o **Physical obstruction**: The robot may be blocked by an object or stuck in its environment.
  - o **Sensor misalignment**: The sensors may not be positioned correctly to detect obstacles or surroundings.
- **Fix**:
  - o Inspect the robot for mechanical issues, such as broken or loose parts, and fix them.
  - o Ensure the robot has enough space to move and that there are no physical obstructions in its path.
  - o Recalibrate the sensors to make sure they are correctly aligned and functioning.

Debugging Python Code for Robotics Applications

When working with robotics, debugging is a critical skill that helps identify and fix issues in the software. Here are some common techniques for debugging Python code in robotics applications:

1. Logging:

- **Log Outputs**: Use Python's `logging` module to print useful information during the robot's operation. This can help track variables, sensor readings, motor states, and execution flow.
- **Example**:

```python
python

import logging
logging.basicConfig(level=logging.DEBUG)
logging.debug("Sensor    reading:    %s",
sensor_data)
```

2. Using Print Statements:

- **Print Debugging**: Adding `print()` statements in the code can help you track the flow of execution and identify where things go wrong.

- **Example**:

```python
python

print(f"Moving to position: {position}")
print(f"Sensor value: {sensor_value}")
```

3. Unit Testing:

- **Test Individual Components**: Use Python's `unittest` framework to write tests for individual parts of your code. This helps ensure that each component functions correctly before integrating them into the full system.
- **Example**:

```python
python

import unittest

class TestRobotMovement(unittest.TestCase):
    def test_move_forward(self):
        robot = Robot()
        robot.move_forward()
        self.assertEqual(robot.position,
1)

if __name__ == '__main__':
    unittest.main()
```

4. Using a Debugger:

- **Interactive Debugging**: Python's built-in `pdb` debugger allows you to step through the code, inspect variables, and set breakpoints. This is useful for more complex issues that cannot be easily diagnosed with print statements.
- **Example**:

```python
import pdb

def move_robot():
    x = 0
    y = 0
    pdb.set_trace()   # Breakpoint
    x += 1
    y += 1
    return x, y

move_robot()
```

5. Profiling:

- **Performance Issues**: Use Python's **cProfile** module to profile your code and identify performance bottlenecks, which are critical for real-time robotic systems.
- **Example**:

```python

import cProfile
cProfile.run('move_robot()')
```

Example: Debugging a Robot That Is Not Responding to Sensor Inputs

Let's say we have a robot that is supposed to move forward until an obstacle is detected by a distance sensor. However, the robot is not responding to the sensor readings. We'll use debugging techniques to identify the problem.

```python

import time
import random

# Robot class with sensor-based movement
class Robot:
    def __init__(self):
        self.position = 0  # Initial position
        self.sensor_value = 10  # Default sensor
reading (distance to obstacle)

    def read_sensor(self):
        # Simulate reading the sensor value
(random distance between 1 and 20)
```

```python
        self.sensor_value  =  random.randint(1,
20)
        print(f"Sensor                 reading:
{self.sensor_value} units")   # Debugging sensor
readings

    def move_forward(self):
        self.read_sensor()   # Read the sensor
before moving
        if self.sensor_value < 5:  # If obstacle
is too close, stop
            print("Obstacle          detected!
Stopping.")
        else:
            self.position += 1
            print(f"Moving   forward.   Current
position: {self.position}")

# Initialize robot
robot = Robot()

# Simulate robot movement for 5 iterations
for i in range(5):
    robot.move_forward()
    time.sleep(1)  # Wait for 1 second before the
next movement
```

Problem: The robot might not be responding as expected, even when an obstacle is present.

Debugging Steps:

1. **Check Sensor Readings**: Add `print()` statements inside the `read_sensor()` method to check if the sensor is providing valid data.
   - o **Solution**: The sensor is working as expected if the readings are within the expected range.
2. **Check Sensor Threshold**: Ensure that the condition `if self.sensor_value < 5` is appropriate for the sensor range and environment.
   - o **Solution**: If the sensor range is between 1 and 20, setting the threshold at 5 is reasonable. However, test different thresholds to ensure the robot responds correctly.
3. **Use Logging**: Add logging to track robot movements and sensor inputs over time.
   - o **Solution**: By reviewing the logs, you can track sensor behavior and robot movements to identify inconsistencies or errors.

Expected Output (with Debugging):

```yaml
Sensor reading: 15 units
Moving forward. Current position: 1
Sensor reading: 8 units
```

230

```
Moving forward. Current position: 2
Sensor reading: 3 units
Obstacle detected! Stopping.
Sensor reading: 19 units
Moving forward. Current position: 3
Sensor reading: 12 units
Moving forward. Current position: 4
```

Conclusion

In this chapter, we explored common errors in robotic systems, focusing on how to troubleshoot and debug code. Whether it's sensor misreads, movement failures, or communication problems, understanding how to identify and fix issues is crucial for developing reliable robotic systems. Python offers several tools, including **logging**, **unit testing**, **debuggers**, and **profiling**, to assist in the debugging process.

We also provided a real-world example of debugging a robot that was not responding to sensor inputs, demonstrating how to use debugging tools and techniques to pinpoint the problem and resolve it. Troubleshooting and debugging are essential skills for anyone working with robotics, helping to ensure that robots perform as expected in dynamic environments.

CHAPTER 25

ADVANCED ROBOTICS TOPICS IN PYTHON

Exploring Advanced Topics like AI Integration, Deep Learning, and Reinforcement Learning

As robotics technology evolves, robots are becoming increasingly intelligent. By integrating **artificial intelligence (AI)**, **deep learning**, and **reinforcement learning** (RL), robots can autonomously learn from their environment, make decisions, and adapt to complex situations. These advanced techniques can greatly enhance the capabilities of robotic systems, enabling them to perform tasks that were once considered too complex or beyond their scope.

1. AI Integration in Robotics:

- **AI in Robotics**: Artificial intelligence allows robots to process and interpret data in a way that simulates human intelligence. This includes tasks such as pattern recognition, decision-making, and problem-solving.

- **Computer Vision**: AI-based computer vision allows robots to understand their surroundings, recognize objects, and navigate through environments. Python libraries such as **OpenCV** and **TensorFlow** are widely used for implementing computer vision tasks in robots.
- **Natural Language Processing (NLP)**: Robots can also use NLP to understand and process human commands or communicate with humans. Libraries like **NLTK** and **spaCy** enable robots to interpret spoken or written language.

2. Deep Learning in Robotics:

- **Deep Learning**: Deep learning algorithms, particularly **convolutional neural networks (CNNs)** and **recurrent neural networks (RNNs)**, have enabled significant advancements in tasks like image recognition, speech recognition, and autonomous driving. Robots can use deep learning to learn features from raw data without explicit programming.
- **Use Cases**:
  - o **Autonomous Navigation**: Deep learning can help robots navigate in dynamic environments by analyzing visual data or sensor data to detect obstacles, plan paths, and make decisions.

o **Object Recognition**: Robots can recognize and classify objects in their environment using pre-trained deep learning models.

o **Facial Recognition**: Deep learning models can enable robots to recognize faces and understand human emotions, allowing for more natural interactions.

3. Reinforcement Learning in Robotics:

- **Reinforcement Learning (RL)** is a subset of machine learning in which an agent learns to make decisions by interacting with its environment. The agent receives rewards or penalties based on the actions it takes, and over time, it learns the best actions to maximize rewards.

- **RL in Robotics**: Robots can use RL to learn complex behaviors through trial and error, such as learning to walk, pick up objects, or navigate through obstacles. RL is particularly useful for tasks that require sequential decision-making and adaptation.

- **Python Libraries**:
  o **OpenAI Gym**: A popular library that provides environments for testing RL algorithms.
  o **Stable-Baselines3**: A Python library for RL, built on top of OpenAI Gym, offering pre-trained models and easy-to-use implementations of RL algorithms.

234

By combining AI, deep learning, and reinforcement learning, robots can be taught to perform tasks that are adaptable to their environment, such as self-learning and autonomous decision-making.

Using Python to Implement Advanced Robotics Algorithms

Python is a versatile and popular programming language in robotics due to its simplicity and extensive support for AI and machine learning. Libraries such as **TensorFlow**, **Keras**, **PyTorch**, and **OpenAI Gym** enable developers to implement advanced algorithms such as deep learning and reinforcement learning.

- **Deep Learning Frameworks**: Python offers several libraries for implementing deep learning algorithms, including:
    - **TensorFlow/Keras**: Widely used for creating and training deep learning models, including CNNs and RNNs, for computer vision and decision-making tasks.
    - **PyTorch**: An alternative to TensorFlow, PyTorch is known for its dynamic computation

graph and is favored by researchers for deep learning projects.

- **Reinforcement Learning Frameworks**: To implement RL, Python offers libraries that make it easy to simulate environments and apply RL algorithms:
  - ○ **OpenAI Gym**: A toolkit for developing and testing reinforcement learning algorithms in a variety of environments.
  - ○ **Stable-Baselines3**: Provides a set of reliable and efficient RL algorithms for use in robotic applications.

With Python's ease of use and robust libraries, it has become the go-to language for implementing advanced robotics algorithms.

Example: Programming a Robot to Learn Through Reinforcement Learning

In this example, we will simulate a **robot learning to navigate a grid world** using **reinforcement learning**. The robot will use Q-learning, a model-free RL algorithm, to learn the optimal policy for navigating through the grid and reaching a goal while avoiding obstacles.

Step 1: Install Necessary Libraries

bash

```
pip install numpy gym
```

Step 2: Define the Environment

We will use **OpenAI Gym** to create a simple environment for the robot. The environment will be a grid, where the robot has to navigate from a start position to a goal.

python

```
import gym
import numpy as np

# Define the environment: a simple 4x4 grid
class GridWorldEnv(gym.Env):
    def __init__(self):
        self.grid_size = 4  # 4x4 grid
        self.start_pos = (0, 0)  # Start at top-left corner
        self.goal_pos = (3, 3)  # Goal at bottom-right corner
        self.robot_pos = self.start_pos
```

```python
        self.actions = [(0, 1), (0, -1), (1, 0),
(-1, 0)]  # Right, Left, Down, Up
        self.action_space                    =
gym.spaces.Discrete(4)  # 4 possible actions
        self.observation_space               =
gym.spaces.Discrete(self.grid_size           *
self.grid_size)  # 16 possible states

    def reset(self):
        self.robot_pos = self.start_pos
        return self.robot_pos

    def step(self, action):
        # Apply action (move robot)
        move = self.actions[action]
        new_pos = (self.robot_pos[0] + move[0],
self.robot_pos[1] + move[1])

        #  Ensure  robot  stays  within  grid
boundaries
        new_pos = (max(0, min(self.grid_size-1,
new_pos[0])),    max(0,    min(self.grid_size-1,
new_pos[1])))

        self.robot_pos = new_pos
        reward = -1  # Default reward (negative
for each step)
        done = False
```

```
        # Check if robot reached goal
        if self.robot_pos == self.goal_pos:
            reward = 10   # Positive reward for
reaching the goal
            done = True

        return self.robot_pos, reward, done, {}

    def render(self):
        grid       =      np.zeros((self.grid_size,
self.grid_size), dtype=str)
        grid[:, :] = '-'
        grid[self.robot_pos] = 'R'   # Mark robot
position
        grid[self.goal_pos] = 'G'   # Mark goal
position
        print("\n".join(["".join(row) for row in
grid]))

# Create environment
env = GridWorldEnv()
```

Step 3: Implement Q-learning Algorithm

We'll now implement **Q-learning**, a reinforcement learning algorithm, to train the robot to find the best path to the goal.

```
python
```

```python
# Q-learning parameters
alpha = 0.1  # Learning rate
gamma = 0.9  # Discount factor
epsilon = 0.2  # Exploration rate
episodes = 1000  # Number of training episodes

# Initialize Q-table with zeros
q_table         =         np.zeros((env.grid_size,
env.grid_size, len(env.actions)))

# Q-learning algorithm
for episode in range(episodes):
    state = env.reset()  # Reset environment
    done = False

    while not done:
        # Epsilon-greedy action selection
        if np.random.rand() < epsilon:
            action                       =
np.random.choice(len(env.actions))  # Explore
        else:
            action = np.argmax(q_table[state[0],
state[1]])  # Exploit

        # Take action, get new state and reward
        next_state,    reward,    done,    _    =
env.step(action)

        # Update Q-value
```

```
        old_q_value       =       q_table[state[0],
state[1], action]
        future_q_value                            =
np.max(q_table[next_state[0], next_state[1]])
        q_table[state[0],  state[1],  action]  =
old_q_value  +  alpha  *  (reward  +  gamma  *
future_q_value - old_q_value)

        state = next_state  # Move to next state


    # Optionally render the environment every 100
episodes
    if episode % 100 == 0:
        print(f"Episode {episode}")
        env.render()


# Testing the learned policy
state = env.reset()
done = False
while not done:
    action      =      np.argmax(q_table[state[0],
state[1]])  # Choose the best action
    state, reward, done, _ = env.step(action)
    env.render()
    time.sleep(0.5)           #    Slow    down    for
visualization
```

Explanation:

1. **GridWorldEnv**: This is a custom environment that simulates a robot navigating a 4x4 grid. The robot starts at (0, 0) and must reach the goal at (3, 3).

2. **Q-learning Algorithm**: The robot learns to navigate the grid by using **Q-learning**. It starts with a Q-table initialized to zeros, which stores the expected future rewards for each state-action pair. The robot chooses actions based on an **epsilon-greedy policy** (exploration vs. exploitation) and updates the Q-values using the **Bellman equation**.

3. **Rendering**: The render() function displays the grid at each step, with the robot (R) and goal (G) marked.

Step 4: Expected Output

During training, the robot will explore the environment, update its Q-values, and gradually learn to navigate toward the goal. After training, the robot will use the learned Q-values to find the optimal path to the goal, avoiding unnecessary steps.

Conclusion

In this chapter, we explored **advanced robotics topics**, including the integration of **AI**, **deep learning**, and

reinforcement learning into robotic systems. We also demonstrated how to use **Python** to implement advanced robotics algorithms, focusing on using **reinforcement learning** to enable a robot to learn to navigate through a grid world.

By incorporating AI and RL, robots can become more autonomous, adaptable, and capable of performing complex tasks. Python, with its powerful libraries and ease of use, makes it an ideal language for implementing these advanced algorithms in robotics.

CHAPTER 26

APPLICATIONS OF PYTHON IN REAL-WORLD ROBOTICS

Overview of Various Real-World Applications of Python in Robotics

Python is a highly versatile programming language that has become integral in developing robotics applications across multiple industries. Its simplicity, rich ecosystem of libraries, and strong community support make it a preferred choice for robotics developers. Let's explore some real-world applications of Python in robotics, including **manufacturing, healthcare, logistics**, and more.

1. **Manufacturing Robotics**:
    o **Automation**: Python is widely used to program robots that automate repetitive tasks in manufacturing environments, such as assembly, packaging, and material handling. Python's simplicity allows engineers to quickly prototype and implement automation systems.
    o **Industrial Robots**: In industrial settings, Python is used to control robotic arms, coordinate

assembly lines, and perform quality checks. Libraries like **pySerial** help interface with hardware components such as motor controllers and sensors.

- o **Robot Simulation**: Python is also used to simulate robots in virtual environments before they are deployed in real-world manufacturing settings. **Gazebo** and **V-REP** are often paired with Python to model, test, and debug robotic behavior.

2. **Healthcare Robotics**:

- o **Medical Robotics**: Python is used in the development of medical robots, including surgical robots, diagnostic robots, and robotic assistants. These robots can assist in complex surgeries or help doctors monitor patients.

- o **Robotic Prosthetics**: Python is used to control robotic prosthetic limbs, allowing for real-time adjustments and providing users with more natural, human-like movements. The flexibility of Python helps in programming complex control systems needed for such devices.

- o **Robotic Rehabilitation**: In physical therapy and rehabilitation, Python helps develop robots that assist patients with movement exercises. These robots monitor progress and adjust resistance or assistance levels based on real-time feedback.

3. **Logistics and Warehouse Robotics**:

   o **Autonomous Delivery Robots**: Python is used in programming delivery robots that navigate warehouses or deliver packages in urban areas. **ROS** and **OpenCV** are frequently used with Python to handle path planning, navigation, and obstacle detection.

   o **Material Handling Robots**: Python powers robots in warehouses for tasks like picking and sorting items. **Deep learning** models can be used to identify and categorize products, while **RL** algorithms can teach robots how to optimize their routes for picking and packing.

4. **Agricultural Robotics**:

   o **Farm Automation**: Python plays a critical role in automating various agricultural tasks such as planting, watering, and harvesting. Robotics systems can be trained to recognize and manage crops, optimize irrigation schedules, and reduce pesticide use.

   o **Weeding and Harvesting**: Machine learning and computer vision techniques in Python are used to develop robots capable of identifying and

246

removing weeds, improving farming efficiency and reducing labor costs.

5. **Search and Rescue Robots**:

   o **Disaster Response**: Python is used to develop robots for search and rescue operations in disaster zones. These robots are designed to navigate through rubble, detect survivors using sensors, and relay information back to rescue teams. Python's flexibility allows for quick adaptations to handle varying scenarios in disaster environments.

   o **Autonomous Drones**: Drones used in search and rescue operations are often programmed with Python to carry out autonomous flights, capture real-time data, and deliver supplies.

6. **Space Exploration Robotics**:

   o **Mars Rovers**: Robots used in space exploration, such as NASA's Mars rovers, often utilize Python to analyze terrain, process images, and autonomously navigate the planet's surface. Python is used to run simulations on Earth before these robots are deployed in space.

   o **Space Station Robotics**: Robotic arms aboard the International Space Station (ISS) are programmed with Python to perform tasks like maintenance and satellite deployment.

247

Example: Developing a Medical Robotic Assistant Using Python

In this example, we will develop a simple medical robotic assistant that assists doctors by monitoring a patient's vitals and helping with basic diagnostic tasks, such as taking blood pressure and heart rate readings. The robot will be able to interact with the doctor using **speech recognition** and **natural language processing (NLP)** to respond to basic commands and give patient updates.

Step 1: Install Necessary Libraries

bash

pip install pyttsx3 SpeechRecognition pySerial

- **pyttsx3**: Library for text-to-speech conversion.
- **SpeechRecognition**: Library for converting speech to text (for doctor-robot communication).
- **pySerial**: Library to interface with external hardware (e.g., blood pressure and heart rate sensors).

Step 2: Simulate the Robot's Operations

The robot will have basic functions like greeting the doctor, taking patient readings, and responding to the doctor's commands. We'll simulate the sensor readings for simplicity.

python

```python
import pyttsx3
import speech_recognition as sr
import random
import time

# Initialize text-to-speech engine
engine = pyttsx3.init()

# Function to speak text
def speak(text):
    engine.say(text)
    engine.runAndWait()

# Simulate taking blood pressure reading
def take_blood_pressure():
    systolic = random.randint(100, 140)
    diastolic = random.randint(60, 90)
    speak(f"Patient's    blood    pressure    is
{systolic} over {diastolic}.")

# Simulate taking heart rate reading
def take_heart_rate():
    heart_rate = random.randint(60, 100)
```

```python
    speak(f"Patient's heart rate is {heart_rate}
beats per minute.")


# Function to listen for doctor's commands
def listen_for_commands():
    recognizer = sr.Recognizer()
    with sr.Microphone() as source:
        print("Listening        for        doctor's
command...")
        audio = recognizer.listen(source)

    try:
        command                                    =
recognizer.recognize_google(audio).lower()
        print(f"Doctor said: {command}")
        return command
    except sr.UnknownValueError:
        print("Sorry,   I   did   not   understand
that.")
        return ""
    except sr.RequestError:
        print("Sorry, there was an error with the
speech recognition service.")
        return ""


# Main function to simulate medical assistant
robot behavior
def medical_assistant():
```

```
    speak("Hello, Doctor. I am your medical
assistant robot.")
    time.sleep(1)

    while True:
        command = listen_for_commands()

        if "blood pressure" in command:
            take_blood_pressure()
        elif "heart rate" in command:
            take_heart_rate()
        elif "exit" in command:
            speak("Goodbye, Doctor. See you next
time.")
            break
        else:
            speak("Sorry, I didn't understand
that command.")

# Run the medical assistant simulation
medical_assistant()
```

Explanation of the Code:

1. **Text-to-Speech**: The `speak()` function uses the `pyttsx3` library to convert text into speech. This allows the robot to communicate with the doctor verbally.

2. **Sensor Simulation**: We simulate taking **blood pressure** and **heart rate** readings using the `random` module. The robot speaks the readings out loud to the doctor.

3. **Speech Recognition**: The `listen_for_commands()` function listens for commands from the doctor using the **SpeechRecognition** library. The doctor can say commands like "blood pressure" or "heart rate," and the robot will respond accordingly.

4. **Main Loop**: The robot continuously listens for commands and responds with appropriate actions (taking measurements or providing information).

Step 3: Expected Output

The robot will greet the doctor, and the doctor can command it to take the patient's blood pressure or heart rate. For example:

```
nginx
```

```
Doctor says: "blood pressure"
Robot responds: "Patient's blood pressure is 120
over 80."
```

Conclusion

In this chapter, we explored **real-world applications of Python in robotics**, including manufacturing, healthcare, and more. Python's versatility and extensive library ecosystem make it ideal for developing robotics applications that require AI, machine learning, and real-time control.

We also developed a simple **medical robotic assistant** using Python, demonstrating how to integrate **speech recognition**, **text-to-speech**, and simulated sensor readings. This example illustrates how Python can be used to create interactive robots capable of assisting healthcare professionals by taking vital signs and responding to verbal commands.

As robotics continues to advance, Python will remain a key tool in the development of intelligent, efficient, and autonomous robotic systems across various industries.

CHAPTER 27

THE FUTURE OF ROBOTICS WITH PYTHON

Emerging Trends in Robotics and Python's Role in the Future

The field of robotics is evolving rapidly, driven by technological advancements, increased computational power, and innovations in artificial intelligence (AI). Python continues to play a pivotal role in shaping the future of robotics due to its versatility, extensive libraries, and growing adoption across various robotic applications. Let's explore some of the **emerging trends** in robotics and Python's role in each.

1. Autonomous Systems and AI Integration:

- **Trend**: One of the most exciting developments in robotics is the increasing autonomy of robots. With advancements in AI and deep learning, robots are now capable of making decisions, learning from their environment, and operating without human intervention.

- **Python's Role**: Python is widely used in **machine learning** and **reinforcement learning** algorithms, which are essential for training robots to perform tasks autonomously. Libraries like **TensorFlow**, **PyTorch**, and **OpenAI Gym** enable robots to learn from data and interact with their environments.

2. Collaborative Robots (Cobots):

- **Trend**: Cobots are designed to work alongside humans in a shared workspace, providing assistance with tasks such as assembly, handling heavy objects, or performing dangerous tasks. These robots are equipped with sensors, AI, and safety mechanisms to ensure smooth human-robot interaction.
- **Python's Role**: Python is increasingly being used to program cobots, particularly for AI-based tasks like object recognition, motion planning, and collaborative task allocation. Python libraries like **ROS** (Robot Operating System) provide easy interfaces for programming robots to cooperate and share tasks.

3. Robot-as-a-Service (RaaS):

- **Trend**: The growth of cloud computing and edge computing is giving rise to **Robot-as-a-Service (RaaS)**, where robots are rented or leased via the cloud to perform specific tasks. This model allows businesses to scale operations quickly without needing to invest in costly robots.

- **Python's Role**: Python will be central in developing the **cloud-based platforms** that control fleets of robots, ensuring smooth communication and real-time decision-making. Python's compatibility with **cloud services** like AWS, Google Cloud, and Microsoft Azure will enable the integration of robotic fleets for on-demand services.

4. Swarm Robotics:

- **Trend**: Swarm robotics is inspired by the behavior of social animals like ants or bees. Multiple robots work together to perform complex tasks through decentralized control and simple local interactions. This is useful in applications such as search and rescue, environmental monitoring, and warehouse automation.
- **Python's Role**: Python is often used to implement **swarm intelligence algorithms** and **distributed systems** that allow robots to communicate, share information, and collaborate. Libraries like **Pyro** for multi-agent systems and **OpenAI Gym** for simulating robotic behaviors will continue to play a critical role in this space.

5. Robotics in Healthcare and Elderly Care:

- **Trend**: Robotics in healthcare is a rapidly growing field, with robots being used for surgery, rehabilitation, diagnostics, and patient care. There is also a growing trend toward using robots for **elderly care**, assisting with mobility, medication delivery, and companionship.

- **Python's Role**: Python is used in **robot-assisted surgery** and **healthcare robots** that require machine learning, image processing, and real-time monitoring. Libraries like **OpenCV** for computer vision and **scikit-learn** for machine learning are key components in developing robotic systems for healthcare.

6. Advanced Robotics for Space Exploration:

- **Trend**: As space exploration becomes more advanced, robotics will continue to play an essential role in missions to the Moon, Mars, and beyond. Robots are being used to explore distant planets, conduct scientific experiments, and even mine resources.

- **Python's Role**: Python is widely used in the development of **space robotics**, where it is used for robot control, data analysis, and simulation. Python-based frameworks like **ROS** and **VREP** (CoppeliaSim) are essential tools in simulating robotic missions and controlling robotic systems in space exploration.

Career Opportunities and Resources for Advancing in Robotics

The field of robotics is expanding at a rapid pace, and there are numerous career opportunities for those interested in pursuing robotics engineering. Python, with its extensive use in AI, machine learning, and robotics programming, is an excellent choice for those seeking to enter the robotics industry. Below are some career paths and resources for advancing in robotics:

Career Opportunities in Robotics:

1. **Robotics Engineer**:
    o   Robotics engineers design and develop robotic systems for various applications. Python is used in many of the tasks, including sensor integration, motion control, and AI-based decision-making.
    o   Key Skills: Programming (Python, C++, ROS), robot design, machine learning, AI.

2. **Automation Engineer**:
    o   Automation engineers develop systems that automate industrial processes. Python is used for programming robotic arms, conveyors, and sensors in manufacturing and production environments.

- o Key Skills: Python programming, industrial automation systems, process control.

3. **AI and Machine Learning Engineer**:
   - o AI engineers develop algorithms that enable robots to learn from their environment and make autonomous decisions. Python, with libraries like **TensorFlow**, **PyTorch**, and **Keras**, is commonly used in training and deploying machine learning models in robotics.
   - o Key Skills: Python, deep learning, reinforcement learning, computer vision.

4. **Robotics Software Developer**:
   - o Software developers specializing in robotics create the software systems that control robots, including user interfaces, robot behaviors, and sensor integrations.
   - o Key Skills: Python, software development, robotics middleware (e.g., ROS), simulation tools.

5. **Robotics Researcher**:
   - o Robotics researchers work in academia or research labs to advance the field of robotics, developing new algorithms and improving robotic systems. Python is commonly used for testing algorithms and creating simulations.

- o Key Skills: Python, robotics research, algorithm development, machine learning.

Resources for Advancing in Robotics:

1. **Online Courses**:
   - o **Coursera**: Offers courses like "Robotics Specialization" and "AI for Robotics."
   - o **edX**: Offers courses on various topics related to robotics and Python, such as "Introduction to Robotics" and "Advanced Robotics."
   - o **Udacity**: Offers a "Robotics Software Engineer" nanodegree program, where you'll work on real-world projects using Python and ROS.

2. **Books**:
   - o "Python Robotics" by Kuno Hasegawa – A great resource for those looking to use Python in robotics programming.
   - o "Learning Robotics Using Python" by Lentin Joseph – A comprehensive guide to building robotic systems with Python.
   - o "Programming Robots with ROS" by Morgan Quigley – A fantastic resource for learning ROS and Python in the context of robotics.

3. **Online Communities and Forums**:

- ○ **ROS Discourse**: A community forum for discussing ROS-related robotics development, with a wealth of resources and tutorials.
- ○ **Stack Overflow**: A programming Q&A platform where many robotics-related issues are discussed, including Python-based solutions for robotics.
- ○ **Robot Operating System (ROS)**: ROS is a popular platform for robotics development. The **ROS Wiki** and **ROS Answers** are excellent resources for getting help and learning more about using Python for robotics.

4. **Robotics Competitions**:
- ○ Participating in robotics competitions, such as the **FIRST Robotics Competition** or **RoboCup**, provides practical experience in building and programming robots using Python.

Conclusion: Key Takeaways and Next Steps for Aspiring Robotics Engineers

The field of robotics is rapidly growing, and Python continues to be an essential tool for programming robots across various industries. From AI and deep learning to reinforcement learning and real-time control, Python offers a rich ecosystem for developing intelligent, autonomous robotic systems.

Key Takeaways:

- Python's simplicity and extensive libraries make it an ideal language for robotics development.
- Emerging trends such as AI integration, reinforcement learning, and collaborative robots are shaping the future of robotics.
- Python is used extensively in industries like healthcare, manufacturing, and space exploration to power robots and automate tasks.
- The demand for robotics engineers, automation experts, and AI developers is expected to grow, with many career opportunities available for those skilled in Python and robotics.

Next Steps for Aspiring Robotics Engineers:

- Start building your skills by learning Python and robotics frameworks like **ROS**.
- Work on projects that incorporate AI, machine learning, and reinforcement learning in robotics applications.
- Explore online resources, books, and courses to deepen your knowledge in specific areas of robotics.

- Get hands-on experience by participating in robotics competitions or internships to build your portfolio.
- Stay current with emerging trends in robotics and continue learning to remain competitive in this rapidly evolving field.

The future of robotics with Python is incredibly exciting, with limitless potential for developing intelligent systems that can interact with and improve the world around us. Whether you are an aspiring robotics engineer or an experienced developer, there has never been a better time to start exploring the possibilities of robotics.

www.ingramcontent.com/pod-product-compliance
Lightning Source LLC
LaVergne TN
LVHW051441050326
832903LV00030BD/3191